하루 30분, 영어 문해력이 자라는 신문 읽기의 힘

바빠 영어 신문

NEWS TIMES

뉴스 타임스

사회 · 경제

이지스에듀

지은이 | 성기홍(효린파파)

EBS English 대표 강사이자 효린파파e어학원 대표이다. 13년 동안 중·고등학교에서 영어를 가르친 전직 교사이이도 하다. 효린·이준 두 아이의 아빠로서 아이들이 영어에 푹 빠져서 정말 영어를 잘하게 되는 환경을 탐구하고 실천하고 있으며, 이렇게 터득한 영어 코칭 노하우를 '효린파파' 인스타그램과 유튜브 채널을 통해 아낌없이 공유하고 있다. 아이들에게 시험을 치는 용도가 아닌 현실에서 사용할 수 있는 진짜 영어 실력을 키워 주기 위해 《바빠 영어신문 NEW TIMES - 사회·경제편》, 《바빠 초등 영어 일기 쓰기》를 집필했다.

• 인스타그램 @hyorin_papa2   • 유튜브 youtube.com/@hyorinpapa

지은이 | 송수영

세인트폴 루터란 고등학교(Saint Paul Lutheran High School)를 거쳐 미국 UC 어바인(University of California, Irvine)에서 의공학(Biomedical Engineering) 학사 및 석사를 마쳤고, 이후 실리콘밸리에서 글로벌 헬스케어 기업 보스턴 사이언티픽(Boston Scientific)에서 제조 엔지니어로 근무했다. 이공계 기반의 논리적 사고력과 영어 실무 경험을 바탕으로, 현재 효린파파e 영어연구소에서 영어 교육 콘텐츠 개발과 학습서 집필에 집중하고 있다.

감수 | Michael A. Putlack (마이클 A. 푸틀랙)

미국의 명문 대학인 Tufts University에서 역사학 석사 학위를 받은 뒤 우리나라의 동양미래대학에서 20년 넘게 한국 학생들을 가르쳤다. 폭넓은 교육 경험을 기반으로 『미국 교과서 읽는 리딩』 같은 어린이 영어 교재를 집필했을 뿐만 아니라 『영어동화 100편』시리즈, 『7살 첫 영어 - 파닉스』, 『바빠 초등 필수 영단어』 등의 영어 교재 감수에 참여해 오고 있다.

하루 30분, 영어 문해력이 자라는 신문 읽기의 힘

바빠 영어신문 NEW TIMES – 사회·경제 편

초판 1쇄 발행 2025년 7월 18일
초판 3쇄 발행 2026년 2월 20일
지은이 성기홍(효린파파), 송수영   원어민 감수 Michael A. Putlack (마이클 A. 푸틀랙)
발행인 이지연
펴낸곳 이지스퍼블리싱(주)   제조국명 대한민국
출판사 등록번호 제313-2010-123호
주소 서울시 마포구 잔다리로 109 이지스 빌딩 5층(우편번호 04003)
대표전화 02-325-1722   팩스 02-326-1723
이지스퍼블리싱 홈페이지 www.easyspub.com   이지스에듀 카페 www.easysedu.co.kr
바빠 아지트 블로그 blog.naver.com/easyspub   인스타그램 @easys_edu
페이스북 www.facebook.com/easyspub2014   이메일 service@easyspub.co.kr

기획 및 책임 편집 이지혜 | 김경진, 박지연, 김현주   교정교열 안현진   문제 검수 이지은
표지 및 내지 디자인 김세리   조판 김민정   인쇄 미래피앤피   독자지원 박애림, 이세진
영업 및 문의 이주동, 김요한(support@easyspub.co.kr)   마케팅 라혜주

ISBN 979-11-6303-738-5 63740
가격 16,800원

• 이지스에듀는 이지스퍼블리싱(주)의 교육 브랜드입니다.
  (이지스에듀는 학생들을 탈락시키지 않고 모두 목적지까지 데려가는 책을 만듭니다!)

펑펑 쏟아져야 눈이 쌓이듯, 공부도 집중해야 실력이 쌓인다.

학교 선생님부터 영어 전문 명강사들까지
적극 추천한 '바빠 영어 신문 NEWS TIMES'!

아이들의 눈높이에 딱 맞는 영어 신문!

이 교재는 아이들에게 부담스럽지 않은 난이도로 지문이 구성되어 있습니다. 한 기사당 총 4단계로 체계적인 학습을 유도합니다. 독해의 기본적인 내용 이해와 어휘 학습뿐 아니라 올바른 작문과 간단한 토론까지 전반적으로 실력을 다질 수 있습니다.
이 책은 아이들의 영어 실력뿐 아니라 사고의 깊이를 더할 수 있도록 도와줄 것입니다.

이은지 선생님
前 (주)탑클래스에듀아이 영어 강사

다양한 언어 능력을 키울 수 있는 책!

신문과 뉴스에서 다루고 있는 다양하고 흥미로운 주제를 영어로 읽음으로써 어휘력 및 독해 실력 향상을 기대할 수 있고, 빈칸 넣기와 문장 쓰기를 통해 영어 글쓰기 능력도 향상시킬 수 있습니다.
더불어 세상에 대한 이해를 넓힐 수 있으며, 글을 읽은 후 부모님과 함께 서로 의견을 주고받는 시간을 가진다면 글을 이해하는 능력과 비판적 사고력도 기를 수 있을 것입니다.

어션 선생님
기초 영어 강사, '어션영어 BasicEnglish' 유튜브 운영자

영어 문해력을 높이는 신문 읽기!

AI시대 미래 인재에게 필수적인 정보 분석력, 비판적 문제 해결력, 창의적 소통 역량을 기를 수 있습니다.
또한 지문 이해, 문장 구성·글쓰기, 세부 정보 파악, 주제별 토론을 통한 표현력 향상까지 단계별 과정을 통해 균형 잡힌 영어 문해력을 향상할 수 있는 교재입니다.

서지예 선생님
부산 공립 중학교 영어교사 겸 작가, '에듀체리' 유튜브 운영자

영어 실력 향상뿐만 아니라 사고 확장까지!

이 교재는 사회, 경제의 중요한 개념이 담긴 주제의 글을 읽으면서, 자연스럽게 영어 어휘력도 키우고, 세상에 대한 관심과 이해도도 높일 수 있도록 설계되어 있습니다. 특히 STEP 4 〈토론하기〉 활동에서는 관련 주제를 다시 한번 생각해 보고, 여러 입장의 의견을 접해 보면서 공감 능력과 생각을 확장할 수 있는 경험을 할 수 있습니다. 이를 바탕으로 자신의 생각을 나타내는 글까지 쓸 수 있겠어요!

김현숙 선생님
영어 강사, '바빠 초등 영어 리딩' 저자

영어 읽기의 폭이 넓어진다!
《바빠 영어 신문 NEWS TIMES》

원어민이 진짜 쓰는 영어를 접할 수 있어요!

이 책은 영어 교과서나 단어장보다 더 현실적이고 생생한 영어 표현을 배울 수 있어요. 신문 기사에는 우리가 현실 세계에서 자주 쓰는 단어나 문장이 많이 나오거든요. 그래서 진짜 사용하는 영어를 접할 수 있죠!

영어 실력 향상과 배경지식 축적을 동시에!

신문 기사는 어휘, 독해, 영작, 회화를 통합적으로 학습하게 해 줍니다. 영어 신문을 꾸준히 읽으면 자연스럽게 영어 실력이 어휘력, 독해력 등 다양한 영역에서 좋아지고, 긴 글도 부담 없이 읽게 돼요. 게다가 다양한 주제(경제, 사회, 환경, 과학 등)의 기사를 읽으면서 배경지식과 시사 상식도 키울 수 있습니다.

쓸 수 있으면 정확히 이해한 거죠!

눈으로만 읽고 끝낸다면, 지문을 온전히 다 이해했다고 보기 힘들 것입니다. 하나를 읽더라도 제대로 읽고 오래 기억할 수 있도록 이 책은 지문을 읽고 문제를 푼 후, 다시 우리말에 맞게 영어 문장을 쓰도록 구성되어 있습니다. 내가 직접 문장을 쓸 수 있다면 그 문장을 정확히 이해한 것이죠!

또 문장을 논리적으로 정리해서 쓸 수 있도록 구성되어 있어서 글의 구성을 보는 감각도 키울 수 있습니다.

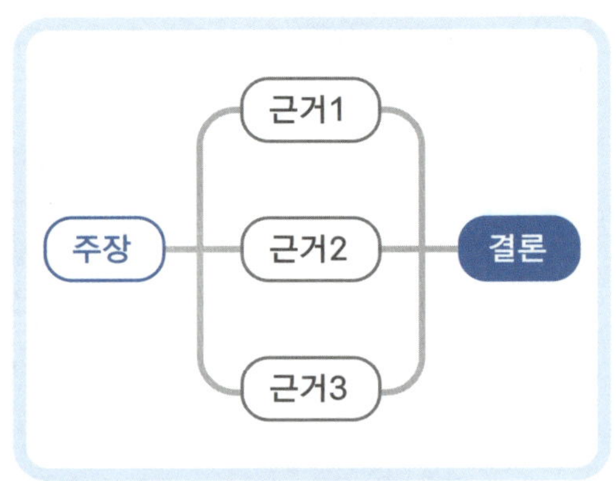

▲ 《바빠 영어 신문 NEWS TIMES》의 논리적인 지문 구성

'4단계 학습법'으로 스스로 영어 신문을 읽을 수 있어요!

영어 신문 읽기가 막막하고 두려운 친구들이라면 이 책의 '4단계 학습법'으로 체계적으로 공부하길 추천합니다!

1단계 **기사 읽기**	영어 신문을 초등학생이 읽을 수 있는 기사로 재구성했어요. 같은 단어가 기사 내에서 반복해서 나오기 때문에 자연스럽게 단어를 익힐 수 있어요. 또 스스로 기사를 읽고 이해할 수 있다는 성취감도 생겨요.
2단계 **확인하기**	STEP 1에서는 기사를 잘 이해했는지 문제를 제공하고 있어요. 1번 문제는 단어 문제, 2번 문제는 내용의 일치&불일치 문제, 3번 문제는 한 줄 요약 문제로 영어 문해력을 키울 수 있어요.
3단계 **기사 쓰기**	STEP 2에서는 앞에서 학습한 기사를 떠올리며 한 문장씩 직접 써요. 기사처럼 논리적인 글쓰기를 훈련할 수 있어요! 혹시 어렵다면 앞 쪽으로 돌아가서 확인하며 진행해도 좋아요.
4단계 **정리&토론**	STEP 3에서는 앞에서 학습한 기사를 요약해서 '주장-근거-결론'으로 다시 정리해요. 그 다음, STEP 4에서는 주제에 대한 찬성과 반대를 생각할 수 있는 토론 학습이 있어요!

Contents

바빠 영어신문 NEWS TIMES – 사회·경제편

1단계 | 신문 읽기

세 번 이상 읽어요!

1회: 눈으로 읽기
2회: 원어민 음원을 들으며 읽기
3회: 큰 소리로 읽기

QR코드를 찍으면 원어민 음원을 들을 수 있어요.

오늘의 지문을 더 잘 이해할 수 있도록 추가 정보를 읽을 수 있어요.

2단계 | 확인하기

세 번 이상 읽었으면 문제를 풀어요!

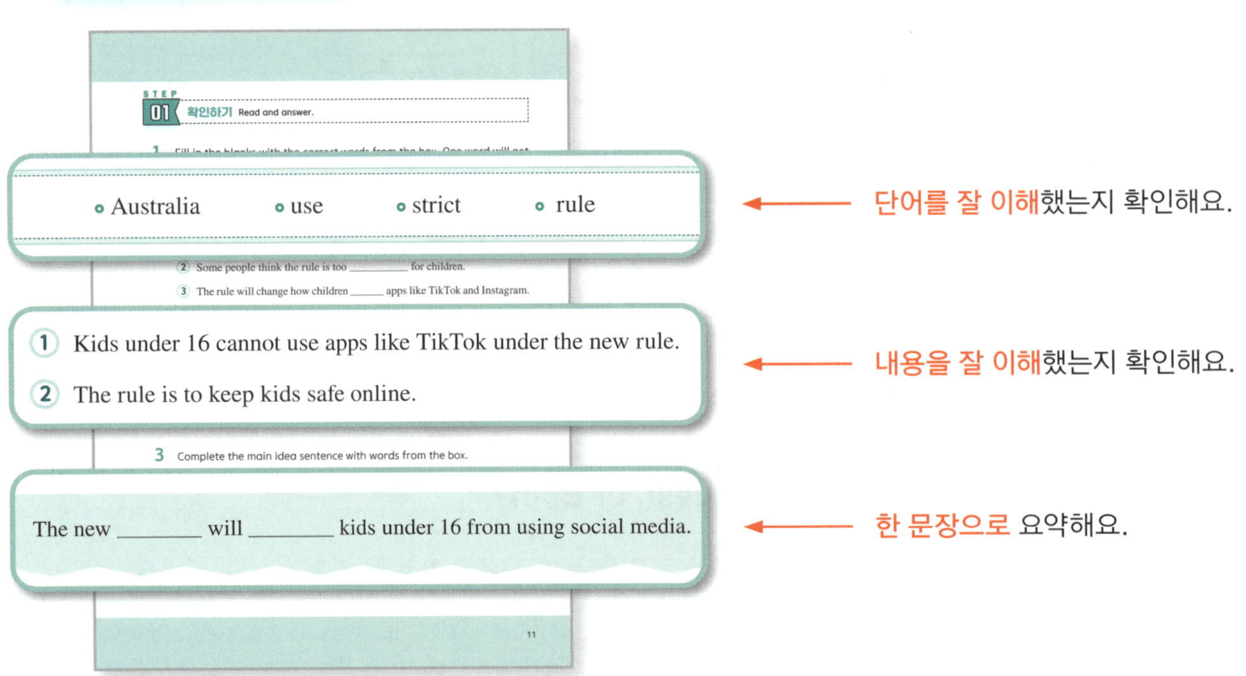

단어를 잘 이해했는지 확인해요.

내용을 잘 이해했는지 확인해요.

한 문장으로 요약해요.

해석을 보며 **영어 작문**을 해 보세요.
어려우면 앞 쪽의 기사를
보고 와도 좋아요.

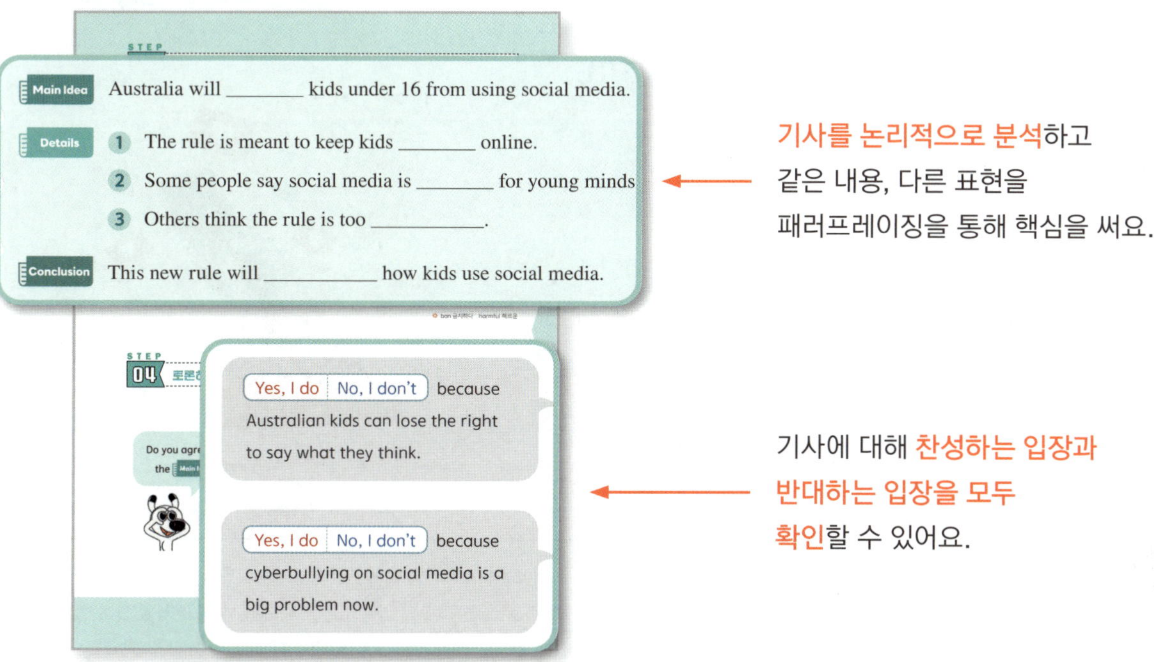

기사를 논리적으로 분석하고
같은 내용, 다른 표현을
패러프레이징을 통해 핵심을 써요.

기사에 대해 **찬성하는 입장**과
반대하는 입장을 모두
확인할 수 있어요.

No More Social Media for Kids!

Word Bank

Australia 호주

social media
소셜 미디어(유튜브,
인스타그램, 틱톡 등)

app 응용 프로그램
(application의 약자)

strict 엄격한

without ~ 없이

permission 허락

fine 벌금

Australia will not let kids under 16 use social media. They cannot use apps like TikTok and Instagram. The rule is to keep kids safe online. Some people say social media is bad for young minds. Others think the rule is too strict. Also, this rule will start without parents' permission. Companies that break this law may get big fines. This new rule will change how kids use social media.

호주의 Online Safety Amendment (Social Media Minimum Age) Act 2024는 16세 미만 어린이들이 소셜 미디어를 사용하지 못하게 하는 법이에요. 이 법은 2024년 11월 28일 호주 국회에서 통과되었고, 2025년 말부터 본격적으로 시행될 예정이에요. 만약 우리나라에도 이런 법이 생긴다면, 친구들은 어떻게 생각하나요?

1 Fill in the blanks with the correct words from the box. One word will not be used.

> • Australia   • use   • strict   • rule

(1) The new _________ does not let kids under 16 use social media.

(2) Some people think the rule is too ___________ for children.

(3) The rule will change how children _______ apps like TikTok and Instagram.

2 After reading the article, circle T(true) or F(false).

(1) Kids under 16 cannot use apps like TikTok under the new rule.   T F

(2) The rule is to keep kids safe online.   T F

3 Complete the main idea sentence with words from the box.

> • stop   • law   • permission   • fine

The new _________ will _________ kids under 16 from using social media.

기사 쓰기 Unscramble the sentences below.

1 use social media / will not let / Australia / kids under 16

호주는 16세 미만 어린이들이 소셜 미디어를 사용하지 못하도록 할 것입니다.

2 like TikTok and Instagram / they / apps / cannot use

그들은 틱톡과 인스타그램 같은 앱을 사용할 수 없어요.

3 is to keep / the rule / safe online / kids

이 규칙은 아이들을 인터넷에서 안전하게 지키기 위한 것이에요.

4 social media / some people say / is bad for / young minds

어떤 사람들은 소셜 미디어가 어린이들(어린 마음)에게 해롭다고 말합니다.

5 the rule is / others / too strict / think

또 다른 사람들은 이 규칙이 너무 엄격하다고 생각해요.

6 will start / also, / without / this rule / parents' permission

또한, 이 규칙은 부모님의 허락 없이 시작될 거예요.

7 big fines / may get / that break this law / companies

이 법을 어기는 회사들은 큰 벌금을 받을 수도 있습니다.

8 how kids / this new rule / will change / use social media

이 새로운 규칙은 아이들이 소셜 미디어를 사용하는 방식에 변화를 줄 것입니다.

← Step 2는 앞 쪽의 기사를 보고 답을 맞춰 보세요.

정리하기 Choose words from the box and complete the organizer.

- strict
- ban
- change
- harmful
- easy
- safe

Main Idea Australia will __________ kids under 16 from using social media.

Details

1 The rule is meant to keep kids __________ online.

2 Some people say social media is __________ for young minds.

3 Others think the rule is too __________.

Conclusion This new rule will __________ how kids use social media.

❋ ban 금지하다   harmful 해로운

토론하기 Choose and circle the correct answers.

Do you agree with the **Main Idea** ?

(Yes, I do | No, I don't) because Australian kids can lose the right to say what they think.

(Yes, I do | No, I don't) because cyberbullying on social media is a big problem now.

❋ right 권리   cyberbullying 사이버 폭력

Taxes: The Price of a Better Life

Word Bank

tax 세금

price 가격

essential 필수적인, 꼭 필요한

medicine 약

depend on 의존하다

important 중요한

exist 존재하다

People pay taxes to help everyone. In Korea, about 40% of tax money is used for essential services. Taxes build schools and pay teachers so children can learn. Taxes also help build hospitals and buy medicine. Many people depend on these important places. For example, taxes pay for police and firefighters. Without taxes, these jobs would not exist. That is why paying taxes is important.

⭐ 우리나라에서는 1년에 500조 원이 넘는 세금이 걷혀요. 하지만 어떤 사람들은 세금이 제대로 쓰이지 않는다고 걱정하고, 일부에서는 세금이 낭비된다고 이야기해요. 그래서 세금을 내는 것도 중요하지만, 그 돈이 어디에 쓰이는지도 관심을 가져야 해요. 친구들은 세금이 어디에 쓰이면 가장 좋다고 생각하나요?

1 Fill in the blanks with the correct words from the box. One word will not be used.

> • firefighters   • schools   • medicine   • hospitals

(1) Taxes help build ____________ where children can learn.

(2) Taxes help buy ____________ for hospitals.

(3) Without taxes, jobs like police officers and ____________ would not exist.

2 After reading the article, circle T(true) or F(false).

(1) Taxes help pay for hospitals and medicine.   T F

(2) Paying taxes is not important.   T F

3 Complete the main idea sentence with words from the box.

> • teachers   • taxes   • exist   • necessary

____________ are ____________ because they help fund schools, hospitals, and jobs.

※ necessary 필요한   fund 자금을 대다

기사 쓰기 Unscramble the sentences below.

1 pay taxes / people / everyone / to help

사람들은 모든 사람을 돕기 위해 세금을 냅니다.

2 for essential services / in Korea, / is used / about 40% of tax money

한국에서, 세금의 약 40%가 필수적인 서비스에 사용됩니다.

3 build schools / taxes / so children can learn / and pay teachers

세금은 학교를 짓고 선생님들에게 월급을 주어 아이들이 배울 수 있도록 해요.

4 and buy medicine / help build hospitals / also / taxes

세금은 또한 병원을 짓고 약을 사는 데 도움이 됩니다.

5 these important places / depend on / many people

많은 사람들이 이러한 중요한 장소들에 의지하고 있어요.

6 pay for / for example, / taxes / police and firefighters

예를 들어, 세금은 경찰과 소방관의 급여를 지급합니다.

7 would not exist / without taxes, / these jobs

세금이 없다면, 이러한 직업들은 존재하지 않을 거예요.

8 paying taxes / that is why / is important

그렇기 때문에 세금을 내는 것은 중요합니다.

← Step 2는 앞 쪽의 기사를 보고 답을 맞춰 보세요.

- support
- worse
- better
- society
- exist
- patients

Main Idea   Taxes help build a better ___________ for everyone.

Details

1. Taxes ___________ schools and teachers.
2. Hospitals use taxes to buy medicine for ___________.
3. Without taxes, important jobs like firefighters would not ________.

Conclusion   Paying taxes makes everyone's lives ________.

☀ support 지원하다   worse 더 나쁜   society 사회

Do you agree with the **Main Idea** ?

AI Is Smart, but People Teach Best

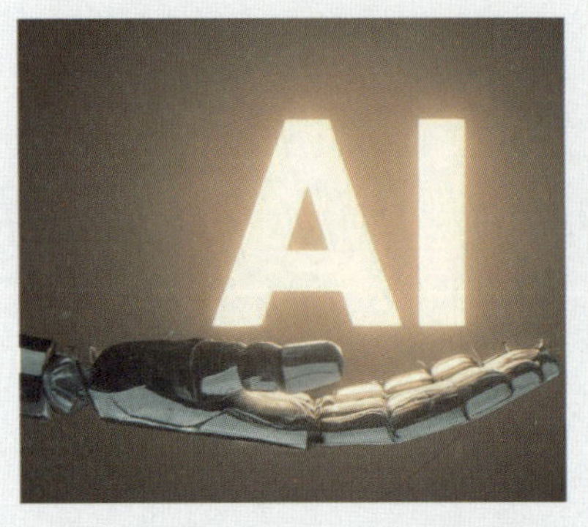

AI, or artificial intelligence, is a smart computer system. It is used in games, robots, online shopping, and more. AI is also used in education but cannot replace people. People understand feelings and support students better. Some say AI makes learning easier and faster. However, AI does not always answer every question correctly. AI still needs more development to teach like people. This is why humans are still the best teachers.

Word Bank

artificial intelligence 인공 지능

education 교육

replace 대체하다

understand 이해하다

support 도와주다

correctly 올바르게

development 발달

지금도 AI는 학교, 병원, 공장, 공항 등 많은 곳에서 쓰이고 있어요. 앞으로 AI가 더 똑똑해지면 일할 수 있는 곳이 더 많아질 거예요. 하지만 AI가 잘 쓰이려면 사람이 바르게 만들고, 올바르게 사용하는 것이 중요해요. 앞으로 AI와 함께 어떤 일을 해보고 싶나요?

STEP

01 확인하기 Read and answer.

1 Fill in the blanks with the correct words from the box. One word will not be used.

development	intelligence	feelings	correctly

① AI, or artificial ________, is used in education but cannot replace teachers.

② AI does not always answer every question __________.

③ Teachers understand students' __________ and help them in a kind way.

2 After reading the article, circle T(true) or F(false).

① AI is used in online shopping, games, and education. T F

② People are still the best teachers because they understand students' feelings. T F

3 Complete the main idea sentence with words from the box.

touch	mistakes	people	understand

AI is smart, but ________ can __________ students better than AI.

mistake 실수

1 or artificial intelligence, / a smart computer system / AI, / is

___

AI, 또는 인공 지능은 똑똑한 컴퓨터 시스템이에요.

2 in games, robots, online shopping, / is used / and more / it

___

이것은 게임, 로봇, 온라인 쇼핑 등 여러 곳에서 사용됩니다.

3 people / AI / but cannot replace / is also used / in education

___

AI는 교육에서도 사용되지만, 사람을 대체할 수는 없어요.

4 feelings / understand / students better / people / and support

___

사람은 감정을 이해하고 학생들을 더 잘 도와줘요.

5 makes learning / AI / easier and faster / some say

___

어떤 사람들은 AI가 학습을 더 쉽고 빠르게 만들어 준다고 해요.

6 does not always answer / however, / AI / every question correctly

___

하지만, AI가 항상 모든 질문에 올바르게 대답하는 것은 아니에요.

7 more development / AI / to teach like people / still needs

___

AI가 사람처럼 가르치려면 아직 더 많은 개발이 필요합니다.

8 the best teachers / humans / this is why / are still

___

그렇기 때문에 인간이 여전히 최고의 선생님이랍니다.

← Step 2는 앞 쪽의 기사를 보고 답을 맞춰 보세요.

 정리하기 Choose words from the box and complete the organizer.

- answers
- feelings
- replace
- useful
- development
- care

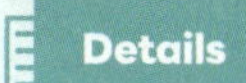

Main Idea AI cannot fully ___________ people in education.

Details

1. Teachers guide students with ________ and understanding.
2. AI cannot understand students' ___________.
3. AI's ___________ are not always correct.

Conclusion AI is __________, but people are still the best teachers.

※ useful 유용한   care 보살핌

 토론하기 Choose and circle the correct answers.

※ support 도움

The Bitcoin Pizza Story

Bitcoin is digital money used for online payments. The first Bitcoin transaction in the real world happened in 2010. A man bought two pizzas with 10,000 Bitcoin. This was the first time Bitcoin was used to buy something. At that time, Bitcoin was very cheap. Today, 1 Bitcoin is worth more than ₩100 million. The day is now called Bitcoin Pizza Day. Bitcoin became more popular after this event.

Word Bank

Bitcoin 비트코인

digital 디지털

payment 지불

transaction 거래

real world 현실 세계

worth ~의 가치가 있는

million 100만

⭐ 비트코인은 최초의 암호화폐(cryptocurrency)예요. 2025년 2월 기준으로, 1비트코인(BTC)의 가격은 약 1.27억 원이에요. 비트코인은 빠르고 편리하지만, 가격이 크게 변하기도 해요. 투자로 손해를 보는 사람도 있어서 조심해야 한다는 의견도 있어요. 정말 비트코인이 돈처럼 쓸 수 있는 좋은 방법일까요?

1 Fill in the blanks with the correct words from the box. One word will not be used.

> ○ worth   ○ pizzas   ○ money   ○ important

(1) The first use of Bitcoin in the real world was to buy __________.

(2) Bitcoin is now ______________ much more than it was in 2010.

(3) Bitcoin Pizza Day became an ______________ moment in Bitcoin's history.

2 After reading the article, circle **T**(true) or **F**(false).

(1) Someone bought two pizzas with Bitcoin in 2010.　　　T　F

(2) Today, 10,000 Bitcoins are worth only a few dollars.　　　T　F

3 Complete the main idea sentence with words from the box.

> ○ history   ○ price   ○ first   ○ digital

Bitcoin Pizza Day is an important day in Bitcoin's __________ because it was the __________ trade using the cryptocurrency in the real world.

❋ trade 거래   cryptocurrency 암호화폐

1 is digital money / Bitcoin / online payments / used for

비트코인은 온라인 결제에 사용되는 디지털 화폐입니다.

2 happened / in 2010 / Bitcoin transaction in the real world / the first

---

첫 번째 현실에서 비트코인 거래는 2010년에 발생했어요.

3 two pizzas / with 10,000 Bitcoin / bought / a man

어떤 사람이 10,000비트코인으로 피자 두 판을 샀어요.

4 this was / Bitcoin was used / to buy something / the first time

---

이것은 비트코인이 무언가를 사는 데 처음으로 사용된 순간이었습니다.

5 was / Bitcoin / at that time, / very cheap

그때 당시에는, 비트코인은 매우 저렴했어요.

6 1 Bitcoin / today, / more than ₩100 million / is worth

오늘날, 1비트코인의 가치는 1억 원이 넘는답니다.

7 Bitcoin Pizza Day / is now called / the day

이 날은 이제 '비트코인 피자 데이'라고 부르고 있어요.

8 became / after this event / more popular / Bitcoin

비트코인은 이 사건 이후 더 유명해졌어요.

← Step 2는 앞 쪽의 기사를 보고 답을 맞춰 보세요.

- popular
- Bitcoin
- value
- purchased
- transaction
- event

Main Idea The Bitcoin Pizza trade was an important ___________.

Details

1. A man ___________ two pizzas with Bitcoin.

2. It was the first Bitcoin ___________ in the real world.

3. The trade showed how ___________ could work.

Conclusion The event helped Bitcoin become more ___________.

※ purchase 구매하다

STEP 04 토론하기 Choose and circle the correct answers.

mukbang 먹방
('먹는 방송'의 줄임말)

follow 따라하다

unhealthy
건강하지 못한

habit 습관

therefore
그러므로

mindfully 주의하여

Enjoy *Mukbang*, but Stay Healthy!

All around the world, *mukbang* is getting popular. *Mukbang* is a video of people eating food. Some people watch it because of the eating sounds. Others watch *mukbang* when they eat alone. *Mukbang* helps people feel less lonely. But thousands of *mukbang* YouTubers eat a lot on camera. This can make people follow their unhealthy eating habits. Therefore, people should watch *mukbang* mindfully.

⭐ 요즘은 먹방을 직업처럼 하는 사람들도 많아요. 먹방을 하려면 음식을 맛있게 먹는 기술, 영상 편집, 말솜씨까지 다양한 능력이 필요해요. 그래서 먹방 유튜버도 하나의 직업으로 볼 수 있어요. 먹방 유튜버가 된다면 어떤 점이 제일 중요하다고 생각하나요?

1 Fill in the blanks with the correct words from the box. One word will not be used.

> ○ unhealthy   ○ alone   ○ mindful   ○ popular

(1) *Mukbang* is getting ____________ all around the world.

(2) Some people watch *mukbang* when they eat ________.

(3) People should be ____________ while watching *mukbang* to stay healthy.

2 After reading the article, circle **T**(true) or **F**(false).

(1) *Mukbang* is a type of video where people eat food. T F

(2) *Mukbang* stars always eat small portions of food. T F

❋ portion (음식의) 1인분

3 Complete the main idea sentence with words from the box.

> ○ careful   ○ sad   ○ habits   ○ sound

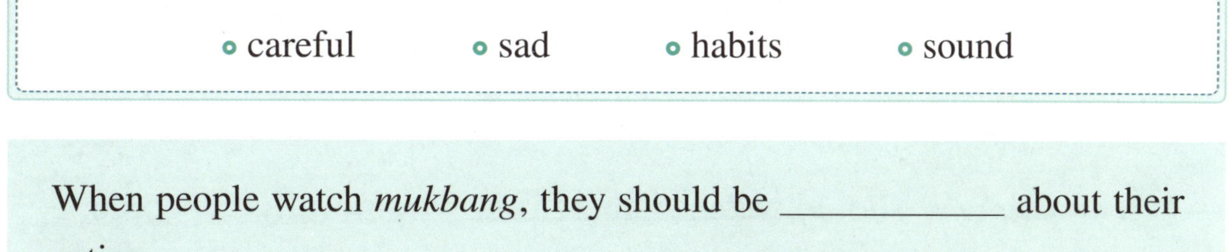

When people watch *mukbang*, they should be ____________ about their eating __________.

❋ careful 조심하는

기사 쓰기 Unscramble the sentences below.

1 is getting popular / *mukbang* / all around the world,

____

세계 곳곳에서, 먹방이 인기를 끌고 있어요.

2 is / *mukbang* / of people eating food / a video

____

먹방은 사람들이 음식을 먹는 영상이에요.

3 watch it / some people / the eating sounds / because of

____

어떤 사람들은 먹는 소리 때문에 그것을 봅니다.

4 watch *mukbang* / others / alone / when they eat

____

다른 사람들은 혼자 밥을 먹을 때 먹방을 봐요.

5 feel less lonely / helps people / *mukbang*

____

먹방은 사람들이 덜 외롭게 느끼도록 도와줍니다.

6 on camera / but / eat a lot / thousands of *mukbang* YouTubers

____

하지만 수천 명의 먹방 유튜버들이 카메라 앞에서 너무 많이 먹어요.

7 people follow / can make / this / their unhealthy eating habits

____

이것은 사람들이 그들의 건강에 좋지 않은 식습관을 따라 하게 만들 수 있어요.

8 *mukbang* / should watch / therefore, / mindfully / people

____

그러므로, 사람들은 주의하며 먹방을 봐야 해요.

← Step 2는 앞 쪽의 기사를 보고 답을 맞춰 보세요.

정리하기 Choose words from the box and complete the organizer.

- enjoyable
- watching
- affect
- helping
- much
- mindfully

Main Idea People should watch *mukbang* ____________.

Details

1. *Mukbang* can make eating more ____________.
2. Many *mukbang* stars eat too ____________ food.
3. Watching *mukbang* can ____________ eating habits.

Conclusion People should be careful when ____________ *mukbang*.

※ enjoyable 즐거운   affect 영향을 미치다

토론하기 Choose and circle the correct answers.

Do you agree with the **Main Idea** ?

※ copy 따라 하다

Word Bank

secondhand
중고의

reduce 줄이다

waste 쓰레기

pollution 오염

landfill 쓰레기 매립

yearly 매년

in addition 또한

unique 특별한

Why Buy New? Shop Smart!

Secondhand shopping is the new shopping trend. Secondhand shopping means buying used things. It is cheaper than buying new things. It also reduces waste and pollution. It reduces landfill waste by 20% yearly. In addition, secondhand stores sell many unique items. People love searching for these special items. That is why secondhand shopping is getting popular.

⭐ 2023년 한 조사에 따르면, 한국 사람 10명 중 6명이 중고 물건을 사본 적이 있다고 해요. 중고 쇼핑 앱 중 '당근마켓'은 한국에서만 1,800만 명 이상이 사용하고 있어요. 그만큼 중고 쇼핑은 더 이상 낯선 일이 아니에요. 중고 쇼핑을 해본 적이 있다면, 어떤 물건을 샀나요?

1 Fill in the blanks with the correct words from the box. One word will not be used.

> ○ waste   ○ cheaper   ○ unique   ○ new

(1) Buying secondhand items is often ____________ than purchasing new ones.

(2) Shopping secondhand can reduce pollution and ____________.

(3) Some people enjoy searching for ____________ items in secondhand stores.

2 After reading the article, circle **T**(true) or **F**(false).

(1) Secondhand shopping is becoming a trend.   T F

(2) Secondhand stores sell only very old and broken things.   T F

3 Complete the main idea sentence with words from the box.

> ○ smart   ○ secondhand   ○ unused   ○ pollution

Shopping ____________________ is a ____________ decision because it is cheaper than buying new things and helps the environment.

※ unused 사용되지 않은   decision 결정   environment 환경

기사 쓰기 Unscramble the sentences below.

1 is / shopping trend / the new / secondhand shopping

중고 쇼핑은 새로운 쇼핑 트렌드예요.

2 means / secondhand shopping / used things / buying

중고 쇼핑은 사용된 물건을 사는 것을 의미합니다.

3 than / buying / it is cheaper / new things

이것은 새 물건을 사는 것보다 더 저렴해요.

4 waste and pollution / also reduces / it

이것은 또한 쓰레기와 오염을 줄여 줍니다.

5 landfill waste / it / by 20% yearly / reduces

이것은 매년 매립 쓰레기를 20% 줄여 줘요.

6 secondhand stores / in addition, / many unique items / sell

또한, 중고 가게들은 독특한 물건들을 많이 팔아요.

7 searching for / love / these special items / people

사람들은 이런 특별한 물건들을 찾는 걸 좋아합니다.

8 secondhand shopping / that is why / is getting popular

그렇기 때문에 중고 쇼핑이 점점 인기를 얻고 있어요.

← Step 2는 앞 쪽의 기사를 보고 답을 맞춰 보세요.

정리하기 Choose words from the box and complete the organizer.

- smart
- cheaper
- reduces
- unique
- spend
- used

 **Main Idea**   Buying __________ items is good for both people and the Earth.

 **Details**

1 Secondhand items are usually __________ than new ones.

2 It __________ waste and pollution.

3 Some items in secondhand shops are __________.

Conclusion   Secondhand shopping is a __________ choice.

❋ purchase 구매하다

토론하기 Choose and circle the correct answers.

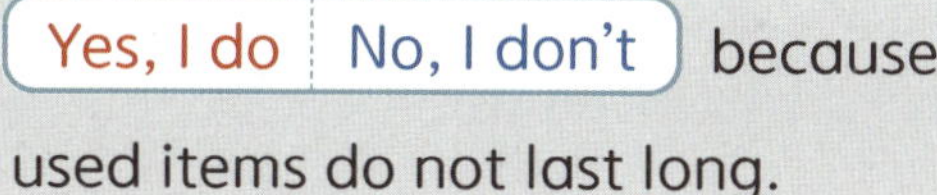

No-Kids Zones: Good or Bad?

Kids are not welcome in some places in Korea. These places are called no-kids zones. According to a recent study, there are over 500 no-kids zones. Some people think this is a good idea. They say it helps adults enjoy quiet time. But others think it is unfair to kids and families. Parents also want places to go with their children. People have different opinions about no-kids zones.

Word Bank

no-kids zone 노키즈존 (아동의 출입 및 이용을 제한하는 곳)

welcome 환영받는

according to ~에 따르면

recent 최근의

adult 어른

unfair 불공평한

different 다른

opinion 의견

☆ 영미권에서는 '노키즈존'을 child-free zone으로 불러요. 한국에는 '노키즈존'으로 운영되는 가게나 공간이 점점 늘고 있어요. 2023년 기준으로 전국에 약 540곳 이상의 노키즈존이 있다고 해요. 반면, 일부 카페나 식당은 '패밀리존(family zone)', '키즈프렌들리존(kid-friendly zone)'처럼 아이들을 환영하는 공간도 따로 마련하고 있어요. 친구들이라면 어떤 공간을 늘리는 게 좋다고 생각하나요?

1 Fill in the blanks with the correct words from the box. One word will not be used.

> • welcome   • children   • unfair   • quiet

(1) No-kids zones help adults enjoy ___________ time.

(2) Some people say these places are ___________ to children.

(3) Children are not ___________ in no-kids zones where adults cannot take their children.

2 After reading the article, circle T(true) or F(false).

(1) No-kids zones are places where only children can go.   T F

(2) Everyone thinks that no-kids zones are a good idea.   T F

3 Complete the main idea sentence with words from the box.

> • peaceful   • fair   • difficult   • unfair

No-kids zones help adults enjoy a ___________ time, but they are not ___________ to children.

※ peaceful 평화로운 fair 공정한

02 기사 쓰기 Unscramble the sentences below.

1 are not welcome / kids / in some places in Korea

____

한국의 몇몇 장소에서는 아이들이 환영받지 못합니다.

2 no-kids zones / are called / these places

____

이러한 장소들을 노키즈존이라고 부릅니다.

3 a recent study, / over 500 no-kids zones / according to / there are

____

최근 연구에 따르면, 500곳 이상의 노키즈존이 있다고 해요.

4 think / a good idea / this is / some people

____

어떤 사람들은 이것이 좋은 아이디어라고 생각해요.

5 they say / enjoy / it helps adults / quiet time

____

그들은 이것이 어른들이 조용한 시간을 즐기는 데 도움이 된다고 말해요.

6 it is unfair / but others think / to kids and families

____

그러나 다른 사람들은 이것이 아이들과 가족들에게 불공평하다고 생각해요.

7 also want / parents / with their children / places to go

____

부모들 또한 아이들과 함께 갈 수 있는 곳을 원해요.

8 about no-kids zones / have / people / different opinions

____

사람들은 노키즈존에 대해 서로 다른 생각을 가지고 있습니다.

← Step 2는 앞 쪽의 기사를 보고 답을 맞춰 보세요.

- different
- take
- same
- adults
- agree
- no-kids zones

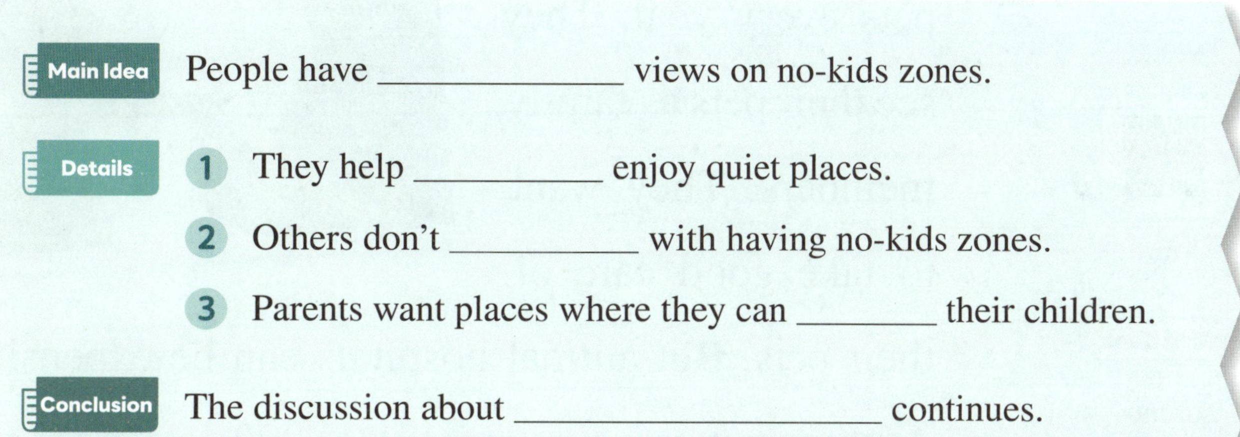

Main Idea — People have _______________ views on no-kids zones.

Details

1. They help __________ enjoy quiet places.
2. Others don't __________ with having no-kids zones.
3. Parents want places where they can ________ their children.

Conclusion — The discussion about ___________________ continues.

※ view 의견   discussion 토론

STEP
04 토론하기 Choose and circle the correct answers.

Do you agree with the **Detail 2** ?

※ right 권리

Pets Need Insurance, Too

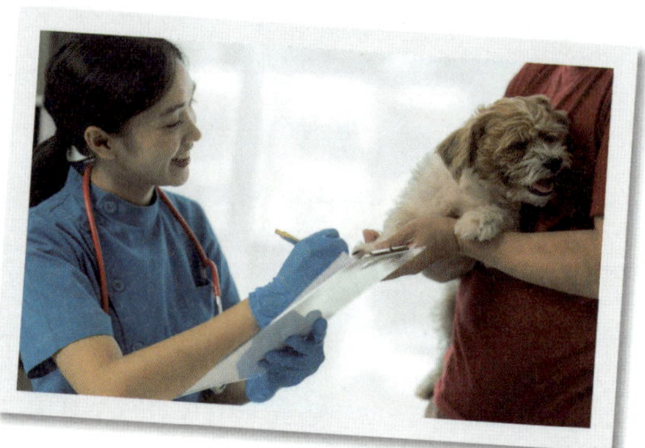

More people are getting pets every year. They see their pets as family members. They want to take good care of their pets. But animal hospitals can be expensive. Average vet care can cost ₩800,000 a year per pet. Luckily, pet insurance helps pay for them. It also helps pets get treatment quickly. That is why more people are choosing pet insurance.

⭐ 요즘 반려동물을 키우는 사람들이 정말 많아졌어요. 2023년 기준으로, 우리나라에서 반려동물을 키우는 가구는 약 600만 가구에 달해요. 이는 전체 가구의 약 1/4에 해당해요. 이렇게 많은 사람들이 반려동물을 키우는 이유는 무엇일까요?

1 Fill in the blanks with the correct words from the box. One word will not be used.

> ○ average   ○ expensive   ○ family   ○ quickly

(1) Many people see their pets as part of their ___________.

(2) Vet care can be very ___________.

(3) Pet insurance helps pets get treatment ___________.

2 After reading the article, circle T(true) or F(false).

(1) Pet insurance helps pay for vet care when pet owners get sick.   T   F

(2) All pet owners buy pet insurance.   T   F

3 Complete the main idea sentence with words from the box.

> ○ risky   ○ choosing   ○ smart   ○ expensive

More pet owners are ___________ pet insurance as a ___________ investment in their pets' health.

※ risky 위험한   investment 투자

기사 쓰기 Unscramble the sentences below.

1 are getting / more people / every year / pets

____

매년 더 많은 사람들이 반려동물을 키우고 있어요.

2 see / they / as family members / their pets

____

그들은 그들의 반려동물을 가족 구성원으로 봅니다.

3 want / their pets / to take good care of / they

____

그들은 그들의 반려동물을 잘 돌보고 싶어해요.

4 expensive / can be / animal hospitals / but

____

하지만 동물 병원은 비쌀 수도 있어요.

5 per pet / average vet care / ₩800,000 a year / can cost

____

평균적인 동물 병원 진료비는 반려동물 한 마리당 1년에 80만 원이 들 수 있어요.

6 pay for them / pet insurance / luckily, / helps

____

다행히도, 반려동물 보험은 진료비를 지불하도록 도와줍니다.

7 also helps / get treatment quickly / pets / it

____

이것은 반려동물이 빨리 치료를 받을 수 있게도 해 줘요.

8 pet insurance / more people / that is why / are choosing

____

그렇기 때문에 더 많은 사람들이 반려동물 보험을 선택하고 있습니다.

← Step 2는 앞 쪽의 기사를 보고 답을 맞춰 보세요.

정리하기 Choose words from the box and complete the organizer.

- medical
- take care of
- quickly
- vet care
- expensive
- insurance

Main Idea Pet insurance helps pet owners pay for _______________.

Details

1. Pet owners want to _______________ their pets.

2. Pet insurance makes _______________ care more affordable.

3. It allows pets to get treatment _______________.

Conclusion More people are choosing pet _______________ today.

※ affordable (가격을) 감당할 수 있는

토론하기 Choose and circle the correct answers.

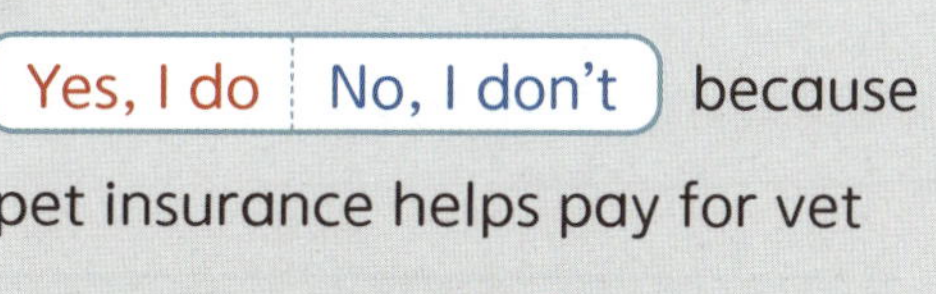

Will Schools Have Fewer Tests?

In Korea, students have many tests at school and academies. In a survey, seven out of ten Korean students feel stress from tests. Too much stress is not healthy for students. That is why some people say fewer tests are better. Some schools are already trying new ways to test students. Projects and essays can replace exams. Experts say this can help students learn better. The future of testing may change in Korea.

Word Bank

fewer 더 적은

academy 학원

survey 조사

way 방법

essay 글, 에세이

exam 시험
(examination의 줄임말)

expert 전문가

OECD(the Organization for Economic Cooperation and Development, 경제협력개발기구)에 따르면, 시험 외에 프로젝트, 포트폴리오, 실습 평가 같은 다양한 평가 방법이 점점 더 중요해지고 있다고 해요. 친구들은 시험 말고 어떤 방식으로 자신의 실력을 보여주고 싶나요? 참고로 OECD는 주로 교육, 경제, 복지 등의 분야에 대해 조사하고 더 나은 정책을 함께 고민하는 국제기구로, 우리나라도 OECD 회원국이죠.

확인하기 Read and answer.

1 Fill in the blanks with the correct words from the box. One word will not be used.

(1) Too many _____________ can make students feel stressed at school.

(2) Having too much stress is not _______________ for students.

(3) Some people think fewer tests are _____________ for students.

2 After reading the article, circle T(true) or F(false).

(1) Most Korean students take few tests. T F

(2) Some schools are already testing students in different ways. T F

3 Complete the main idea sentence with words from the box.

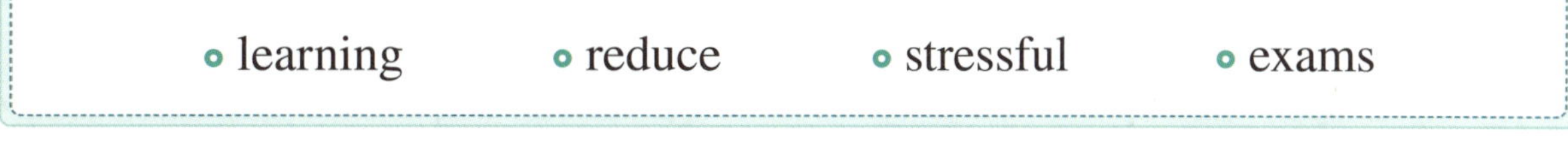

In the future, schools might _____________ the number of ___________ students have to take.

✳ reduce 줄이다   stressful 스트레스가 많은

1 at school and academies / many tests / have / students / in korea,

____

한국에, 학생들은 학교와 학원에서 시험을 많이 봐요.

2 from tests / Korean students / seven out of ten / feel stress / in a survey,

____

조사에서, 한국 학생 10명 중 7명이 시험으로 스트레스를 느껴요.

3 for students / is not healthy / too much stress

____

지나친 스트레스는 학생들의 건강에 좋지 않아요.

4 some people say / are better / fewer tests / that is why

____

그렇기 때문에 어떤 사람들은 시험을 줄이는 것이 낫다고 말해요.

5 are already trying / some schools / to test students / new ways

____

일부 학교에서는 이미 학생들을 평가하는 새로운 방법들을 시도하고 있어요.

6 can replace / exams / projects and essays

____

프로젝트와 에세이가 시험을 대신할 수 있지요.

7 learn better / can help / this / students / experts say

____

전문가들은 이것이 학생들이 더 잘 배우는 데 도움이 될 수 있다고 말해요.

8 in Korea / may change / the future of testing

____

한국에서 시험의 미래가 달라질 수도 있어요.

← Step 2는 앞 쪽의 기사를 보고 답을 맞춰 보세요.

정리하기 **Choose words from the box and complete the organizer.**

- methods
- fewer
- essays
- unhealthy
- enjoy
- replace

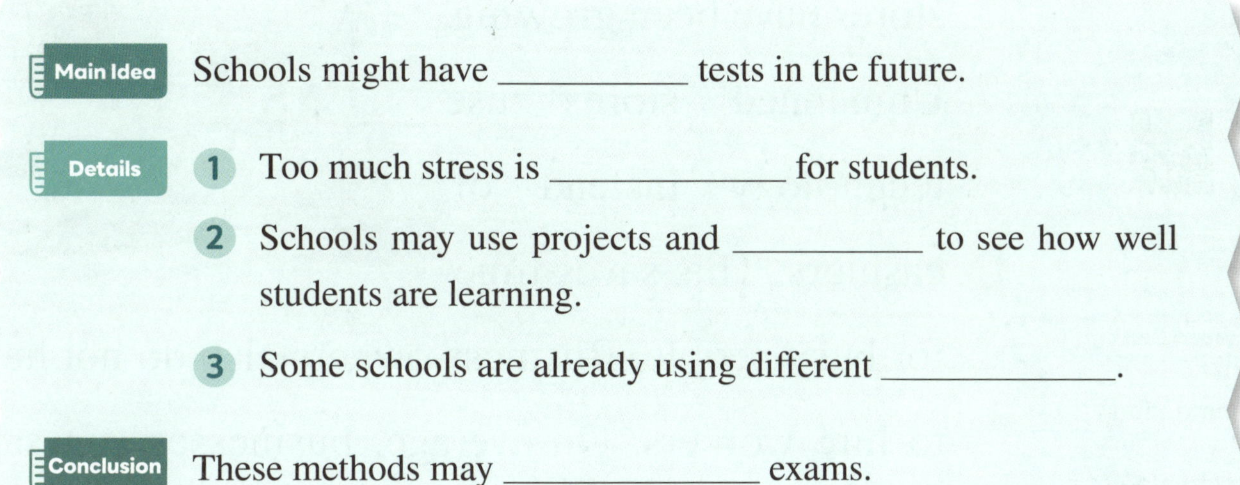

Main Idea   Schools might have ___________ tests in the future.

Details

1. Too much stress is ___________ for students.
2. Schools may use projects and ___________ to see how well students are learning.
3. Some schools are already using different ___________.

Conclusion   These methods may ___________ exams.

✻ method 방법

STEP
04

토론하기 **Choose and circle the correct answers.**

Do you agree with the Main Idea ?

✻ focus 집중하다   memorize 암기하다

No Cashier? No Problem?

In recent years, unmanned stores have been growing. Unmanned stores use technology instead of cashiers. This saves time for busy people. Business owners also do not have to hire workers. On average, businesses can save millions of won each year. But cashiers may lose their jobs. Older people may not understand the new technology. Unmanned stores are convenient, but they are not for everyone.

Word Bank

unmanned 무인의

technology 기술

instead of ~ 대신

cashier 계산대 점원

business 사업

hire 고용하다

convenient 편리한

⭐ 무인 매장에서는 QR코드, 키오스크, 앱 결제 등 다양한 기술이 사용돼요. 하지만 이런 기술을 이용해 본 55세 이상 고령층 중 약 60%는 사용하는 데 어려움을 느낀다고 해요. 이런 불편함을 줄이기 위해, 안내 요원을 배치하거나 쉬운 화면을 만드는 노력도 필요해요. 친구들이라면 어르신들이 무인 매장을 더 쉽게 이용할 수 있도록 어떤 아이디어를 낼 수 있을까요?

확인하기 Read and answer.

1 Fill in the blanks with the correct words from the box. One word will not be used.

> ○ technology   ○ hire   ○ unmanned   ○ convenient

① _________________ stores do not have cashiers.

② Instead of cashiers, people use _________________ to pay.

③ These stores are _________________ for people with busy lives.

2 After reading the article, circle **T**(true) or **F**(false).

① Some older people may not understand the new system.   T   F

② Business owners can save money because they do not have to hire workers.   T   F

3 Complete the main idea sentence with words from the box.

> ○ cashiers   ○ business   ○ stores   ○ magic

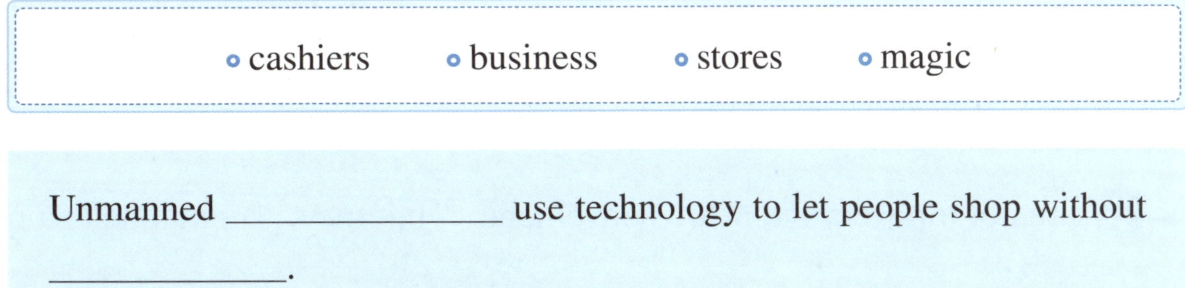

Unmanned _________________ use technology to let people shop without _________________.

1 have been growing / unmanned stores / in recent years,

최근 몇 년 사이에, 무인 매장이 점점 늘어나고 있어요.

2 instead of cashiers / unmanned stores / technology / use

무인 매장은 계산대 점원 대신 기술을 사용해요.

3 time / for busy people / this / saves

이것은 바쁜 사람들의 시간을 절약해 줍니다.

4 business owners / hire / also do not have to / workers

가게 주인들은 또한 직원을 고용하지 않아도 됩니다.

5 can save / on average, / each year / millions of won / businesses

평균적으로, 가게들은 매년 수백만 원을 아낄 수 있어요.

6 cashiers / their jobs / may lose / but

하지만 계산원들은 그들의 일자리를 잃을 수도 있어요.

7 the new technology / may not understand / older people

나이가 많으신 분들이 새로운 기술을 이해하지 못할 수도 있어요.

8 are not for everyone / are convenient, / but they / unmanned stores

무인 매장은 편리하지만, 그것들은 모든 사람에게 좋은 것은 아니에요.

← Step 2는 앞 쪽의 기사를 보고 답을 맞춰 보세요.

정리하기 Choose words from the box and complete the organizer.

- customers
- cashiers
- different
- owners
- faster
- prefer

 **Main Idea** Unmanned stores use technology instead of ________________.

Details

1 They make shopping ___________.

2 Business ___________ do not need to hire cashiers.

3 However, some people _____________ the old system.

Conclusion People have _____________ opinions about unmanned stores.

※ customer 손님　prefer 선호하다　system 시스템

토론하기 Choose and circle the correct answers.

 Do you agree with the **Main Idea** ?

※ in line 줄을 서서

Zoo: Safe Homes or Small Prisons?

Word Bank

prison 감옥

care 관심

right 권리

attention 주목

protect 보호하다

endangered 멸종 위기에 처한

grow in number 수가 늘어나다

public 공립의

private 사립의

chance 기회

Growing care for animals' rights brings more attention to zoos. Zoos help protect endangered animals from harm. Zoos help them grow in number. In Korea, there are 127 zoos, including both public and private ones. These zoos give kids the chance to learn about animals. But some people believe animals should not live in zoos. They may not feel free and may get stressed. People have different opinions about zoos.

우리나라에는 서울대공원, 대전오월드, 에버랜드처럼 다양한 동물원이 있어요. 하지만 2023년 기준으로, 등록되지 않은 사설 동물원이 전체의 절반 이상을 차지한다고 해요. 이렇게 등록되지 않은 동물원들 중에 동물들이 잘 지낼 수 있도록 지켜야 할 기본 규칙을 지키지 않는 곳도 있다고 해요. 친구들은 동물원이 어떤 기준을 지켜야 한다고 생각하나요?

STEP 01

확인하기 Read and answer.

1 Fill in the blanks with the correct words from the box. One word will not be used.

(1) More people care about animal ___________ today.

(2) Zoos help keep endangered ___________ safe.

(3) These places let kids ________ about animals.

2 After reading the article, circle **T**(true) or **F**(false).

(1) Some people think animals feel stressed in zoos.   T   F

(2) All people think animals should live in zoos.   T   F

3 Complete the main idea sentence with words from the box.

Zoos are getting more ______________ as more people __________ about animal rights.

1 brings / for animals' rights / to zoos / growing care / more attentions

———————————————————————————

동물의 권리에 대한 커져 가는 관심은 동물원에 더 많은 관심을 가져 옵니다.

2 help protect / zoos / from harm / endangered animals

———————————————————————————

동물원은 멸종 위기에 처한 동물들을 해로움으로부터 보호하는 데 도움을 줍니다.

3 grow in number / help them / zoos

———————————————————————————

동물원은 그들의 수가 늘어나도록 도와줍니다.

4 including / there are / both public and private ones / 127 zoos, / in korea

———————————————————————————

한국에, 공립과 사립 둘 다 포함해서, 127개의 동물원이 있어요.

5 give kids / about animals / the chance to learn / these zoos

———————————————————————————

이 동물원들은 아이들이 동물들에 대해 배울 수 있는 기회를 줍니다.

6 some people believe / but / animals / in zoos / should not live

———————————————————————————

하지만 어떤 사람들은 동물들은 동물원에서 살아서는 안 된다고 믿어요.

7 may not / they / and may get stressed / feel free

———————————————————————————

그들은 자유롭지 않다고 느낄 수도 있고 스트레스를 받을 수도 있어요.

8 have / about zoos / people / different opinions

———————————————————————————

사람들은 동물원에 대해 서로 다른 생각을 가지고 있어요.

← Step 2는 앞 쪽의 기사를 보고 답을 맞춰 보세요.

정리하기 Choose words from the box and complete the organizer.

- different
- protect
- free
- stressed
- disagree
- learn

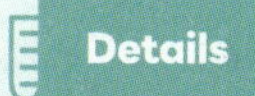 **Main Idea** People share ______________ opinions about zoos.

Details
1 Zoos ______________ endangered animals from danger.
2 Kids visit zoos to ___________ about animals.
3 Some people worry that animals feel __________ in zoos.

Conclusion Some people agree, but others ______________ about zoos.

※ disagree 동의하지 않다

토론하기 Choose and circle the correct answers.

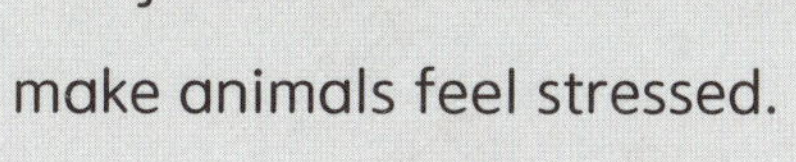

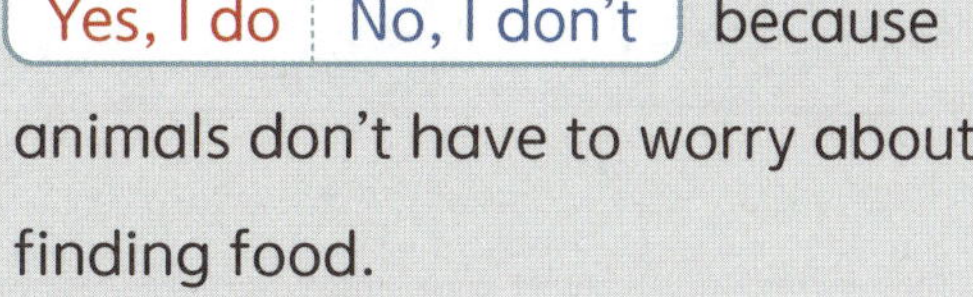

Word Bank

Jeonse 전세

option 선택지

housing system
주거 시스템

rent 집세

move out
이사 나가다

homeowner 집주인

investment 투자

renter 세입자

Why Do People Use *Jeonse*?

It's getting harder to buy a home in Korea. One popular option is *Jeonse*, a unique housing system. People do not have to pay rent every month. Instead, they pay a lot of money at the beginning. However, they get their money back when they move out. It also gives the homeowners money for investments. *Jeonse* helps both homeowners and renters. This is why many people choose *Jeonse*.

⭐ 전세는 한국에만 있는 독특한 주거 방식이에요. 하지만 최근 몇 년 동안 전세 보증금이 크게 올라서 세입자들의 부담이 커졌어요. 또 전세 사기를 걱정하는 사람들도 많아졌어요. 그래서 정부는 보증보험이나 전세 사기 예방 책을 만들고 있어요. 친구들은 전세 제도가 어떻게 바뀌면 좋겠다고 생각하나요?

1 Fill in the blanks with the correct words from the box. One word will not be used.

> ○ end　　○ beginning　　○ unique　　○ renters

1 *Jeonse* is a ____________ housing system in Korea.

2 Renters give a big amount of money at the ______________.

3 ____________ get their money back when they move out.

2 After reading the article, circle **T**(true) or **F**(false).

1 In Korea, it is getting easier to buy a home. 　　T　F

2 With *Jeonse*, people pay rent every month. 　　T　F

3 Complete the main idea sentence with words from the box.

> ○ monthly rent　　○ homeowners　　○ *Jeonse*　　○ option

Many people choose ______________ because it helps both renters and ______________.

❋ monthly rent 월세

기사 쓰기 Unscramble the sentences below.

1 to buy / in Korea / a home / it's getting harder

____

한국에서 집을 사는 것이 점점 더 어려워지고 있어요.

2 is / one popular option / a unique housing system / *Jeonse*,

____

인기 있는 선택지 중 하나는 전세라는 독특한 주거 시스템입니다.

3 rent / people / every month / do not have to pay

____

사람들은 매달 집세를 내지 않아도 돼요.

4 they / instead, / a lot of money / at the beginning / pay

____

대신, 그들은 처음에 많은 돈을 내요.

5 get / they / when they move out / their money back / however,

____

하지만, 그들은 이사를 나갈 때 그들의 돈을 돌려받아요.

6 the homeowners / it / money for investments / also gives

____

이것은 집주인에게 투자를 위한 돈을 주기도 합니다.

7 helps / *Jeonse* / homeowners and renters / both

____

전세는 집주인과 세입자 둘 다에게 도움이 됩니다.

8 choose / *Jeonse* / many people / this is why

____

그렇기 때문에 많은 사람들이 전세를 선택해요.

← Step 2는 앞 쪽의 기사를 보고 답을 맞춰 보세요.

정리하기 Choose words from the box and complete the organizer.

- option
- monthly
- renters
- rent
- investments
- *Jeonse*

Main Idea The *Jeonse* housing system helps both ________ and homeowners.

Details

1 *Jeonse* is a housing system without ____________ rent.

2 Renters don't have to pay __________ every month.

3 *Jeonse* also gives the homeowners money for ____________.

Conclusion For this reason, many people choose __________.

※ monthly 매달의

토론하기 Choose and circle the correct answers.

Do you agree with the Main Idea **?**

※ run away 도망가다

Do You Want to Be a YouTuber?

A recent survey says over 40% of kids want to be YouTubers. They like making videos and sharing their hobbies. Some YouTubers make a lot of money, too. Top kid YouTubers make billions of won every year. But making videos takes a lot of time. Some YouTubers feel tired or stressed. Cyberbullying is also a big problem for them. That's why kids should think carefully before becoming YouTubers.

게임, 장난감, 요리 등을 소재로 자신만의 콘텐츠를 만들고 싶어 하는 아이들이 많아졌어요. 10살 유튜버 '보람튜브'는 수십억 원을 벌어 큰 화제가 되기도 했어요. 유튜버는 재미있고 멋져 보이지만, 꾸준히 영상을 만들고 악플을 이겨내야 해요. 친구들이 유튜버가 된다면, 즐거움과 책임감 중 어떤 것이 더 중요하다고 생각하나요?

1 Fill in the blanks with the correct words from the box. One word will not be used.

> ◦ videos ◦ money ◦ hobbies ◦ YouTubers

(1) A recent survey says many kids want to be ________________.

(2) They enjoy showing their ____________ in their videos.

(3) Making good ____________ takes a lot of time.

2 After reading the article, circle **T**(true) or **F**(false).

(1) Fewer than 4% of kids want to be YouTubers. T F

(2) Cyberbullying can be a problem for YouTubers. T F

3 Complete the main idea sentence with words from the box.

> ◦ cyberbullying ◦ after ◦ being ◦ before

____________ a YouTuber is not easy, so kids should think carefully ____________ they choose to become YouTubers.

기사 쓰기 Unscramble the sentences below.

1 over 40% of kids / want to be / a recent survey says / YouTubers

____

최근 연구에 따르면 40% 이상의 아이들이 유튜버가 되고 싶어 합니다.

2 like / they / and sharing their hobbies / making videos

____

그들은 영상 만들기와 그들의 취미를 공유하는 것을 좋아해요.

3 a lot of money, too / make / some YouTubers

____

어떤 유튜버들은 돈도 많이 벌어요.

4 billions of won / every year / make / top kid YouTubers

____

상위권 어린이 유튜버들은 매년 수십억을 벌기도 해요.

5 a lot of time / making videos / but / takes

____

하지만 영상을 만드는 데는 많은 시간이 들어요.

6 feel tired / some YouTubers / or stressed

____

어떤 유튜버들은 피곤하거나 스트레스를 느낍니다.

7 is also / cyberbullying / for them / a big problem

____

사이버 폭력도 그들에게 큰 문제입니다.

8 kids should think / before becoming YouTubers / that's why / carefully

____

그래서 아이들은 유튜버가 되기 전에 신중히 생각해야 해요.

← Step 2는 앞 쪽의 기사를 보고 답을 맞춰 보세요.

- carefully
- easy
- difficult
- videos
- bully
- stressed

Main Idea Being a YouTuber is fun but not always an __________ job.

Details

1. Making ______________ looks fun to many kids.

2. But making videos takes a lot of time, so they can feel ______________.

3. Other people may also _________ the kids online.

Conclusion That's why kids must think ________________ before becoming a YouTuber.

※ bully 괴롭히다

Do you agree with the **Main Idea**?

(Yes, I do | No, I don't) because they need to think of fun ideas all the time.

(Yes, I do | No, I don't) because doing what you love should make it feel easy.

Brands: More Than Just a Name

Word Bank

brand 브랜드

researcher 연구자

image 이미지

affect 영향을 미치다

modern 현대적인

sporty 스포츠를 잘하는

spend (돈을) 쓰다
(과거형은 spent)

trillion 1조

ad 광고
(advertising의 약자)

Researchers say brand images affect what people buy. Brand images help people show who they are. Some people like Apple for its smart, modern image. Some people buy Nike for its strong, sporty image. People buy from brands with images they like. This is why brands work hard to make good images. For example, Apple and Nike spent trillions of won on ads in 2023. This shows how important brand images are.

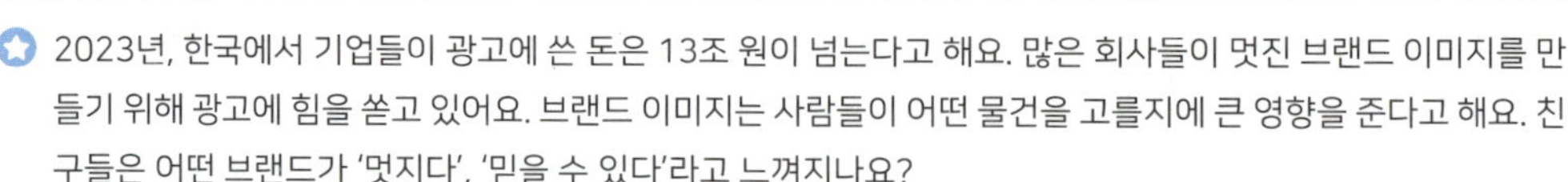

❇ 2023년, 한국에서 기업들이 광고에 쓴 돈은 13조 원이 넘는다고 해요. 많은 회사들이 멋진 브랜드 이미지를 만들기 위해 광고에 힘을 쏟고 있어요. 브랜드 이미지는 사람들이 어떤 물건을 고를지에 큰 영향을 준다고 해요. 친구들은 어떤 브랜드가 '멋지다', '믿을 수 있다'라고 느껴지나요?

1 Fill in the blanks with the correct words from the box. One word will not be used.

(1) Researchers say brand images affect what people ____________.

(2) People choose brands that show ________ they are.

(3) Big brands spend a lot of money on ____________.

2 After reading the article, circle **T**(true) or **F**(false).

(1) People buy things only because they are cheap.　　**T**　**F**

(2) Apple and Nike spent trillions of won on ads in 2023.　　**T**　**F**

3 Complete the main idea sentence with words from the box.

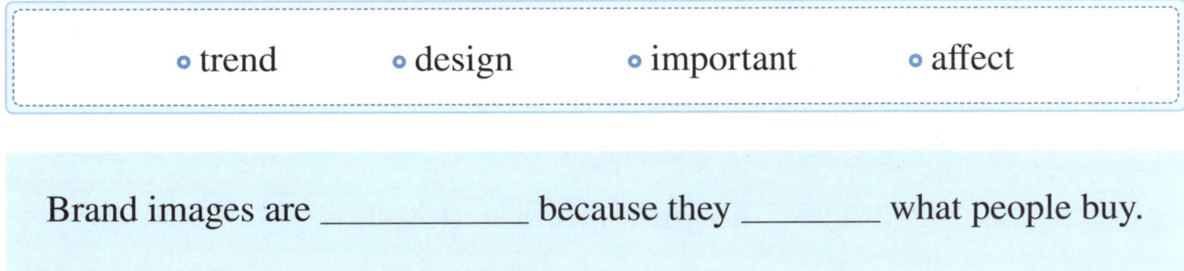

Brand images are ____________ because they ________ what people buy.

❊ trend 트렌드

1 brand images / what people buy / affect / researchers say

연구자들은 브랜드 이미지가 사람들이 무엇을 사는지에 영향을 준다고 말합니다.

2 show / help people / who they are / brand images

브랜드 이미지는 사람들이 그들 자신이 누구인지를 보여주는 데 도움을 줘요.

3 Apple / like / for its smart, modern image / some people

어떤 사람들은 그것의(애플의) 똑똑하고 현대적인 이미지 때문에 애플을 좋아해요.

4 buy / for its strong, sporty image / Nike / some people

어떤 사람들은 그것의(나이키의) 강하고 스포츠를 잘하는 이미지 때문에 나이키를 삽니다.

5 with images they like / people / from brands / buy

사람들은 그들이 좋아하는 이미지를 가진 브랜드에서 사요.

6 brands / this is why / to make good images / work hard

그렇기 때문에 브랜드들이 좋은 이미지들을 만들기 위해 열심히 노력한답니다.

7 trillions of won / spent / Apple and Nike / on ads in 2023 / for example,

예를 들어, 애플과 나이키는 2023년에 광고에 수조 원을 썼어요.

8 brand images are / how important / this shows

이것은 브랜드 이미지가 얼마나 중요한지를 보여줍니다.

← Step 2는 앞 쪽의 기사를 보고 답을 맞춰 보세요.

정리하기 Choose words from the box and complete the organizer.

- what
- logo
- images
- brand
- choose
- money

Main Idea

Brand images affect _________ people buy.

Details

1 People _____________ brands that match who they are.

2 Brands understand this, so they try hard to make good _______.

3 Big brands spend a lot of ____________ to build their image.

Conclusion

_________ images are very important.

토론하기 Choose and circle the correct answers.

Do you agree with the **Main Idea**?

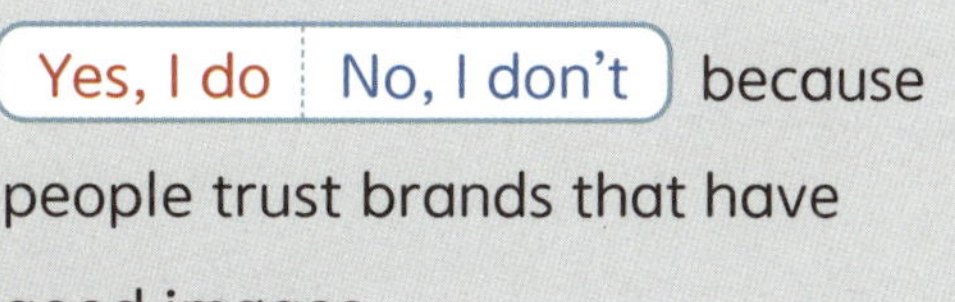

※ quality 품질   trust 신뢰하다

Word Bank

age 시대

matter 중요하다

teamwork 협동

in addition to
~뿐만 아니라

subject 수업 과목

kindness 친절함

respect 존경, 존중

responsible
책임감 있는

member 구성원

employer 고용주

Why Do We Have to Go to School?

In the age of AI, working well with others matters more. At school, children can learn important skills like teamwork. In addition to school subjects, students learn kindness and respect. They listen to others and share ideas. Students can practice these skills in group settings. School also teaches them to be responsible team members. A survey shows that 80% of employers think these skills are important. That's why students should go to school.

⭐ AI가 많은 일을 대신하는 시대이지만, 사람들과 잘 어울리는 능력은 여전히 중요해요. 세계경제포럼(WEF)에 따르면, 2025년까지 가장 중요한 직업 능력 중 하나가 '팀워크와 소통'이라고 해요. 학교에서는 친구들과 팀 활동을 하며 이런 능력을 기를 수 있어요. 친구들은 학교에서 어떤 활동을 통해 팀워크와 소통 기술을 배우고 있나요?

1 Fill in the blanks with the correct words from the box. One word will not be used.

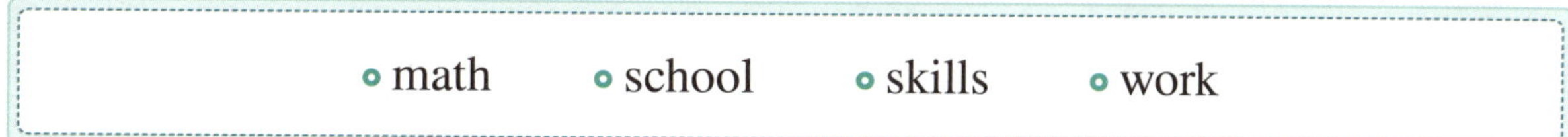

○ math   ○ school   ○ skills   ○ work

(1) ____________ teaches children how to share and listen.

(2) Children can learn useful ____________ at school.

(3) Teamwork helps children ____________ well with others.

2 After reading the article, circle **T**(true) or **F**(false).

(1) Listening to others and sharing ideas are important skills.   T   F

(2) Only 20% of employers think teamwork is important.   T   F

3 Complete the main idea sentence with words from the box.

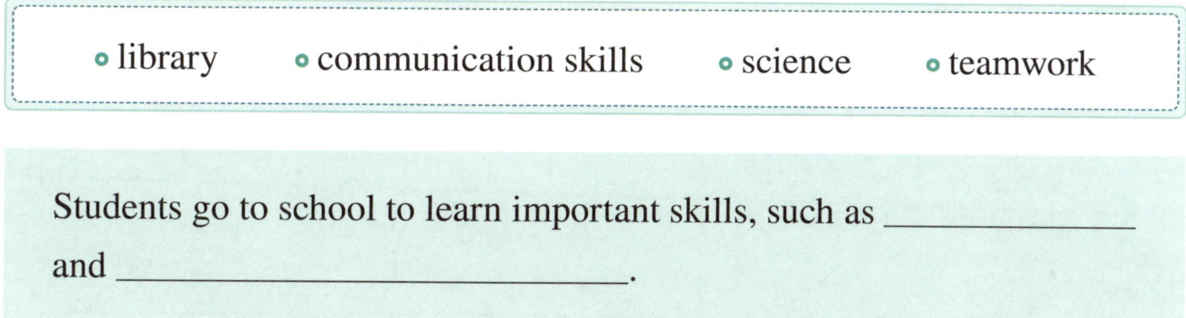

○ library   ○ communication skills   ○ science   ○ teamwork

Students go to school to learn important skills, such as ____________ and ____________.

※ communication 의사소통

1 working well / in the age of AI, / matters more / with others

____

AI 시대에는, 다른 사람들과 잘 협력하는 것이 더 중요해졌어요.

2 children / important skills / can learn / like teamwork / at school,

____

학교에서 아이들은 협동과 같은 중요한 능력들을 배울 수 있습니다.

3 kindness and respect / learn / students / school subjects, / in addition to

____

교과목뿐만 아니라 학생들은 친절함과 존중을 배웁니다.

4 others / they / and share ideas / listen to

____

그들은 다른 사람들의 말을 경청하고 생각을 나눕니다.

5 can practice / students / in group settings / these skills

____

학생들은 이런 기술들을 단체 환경 속에서 연습할 수 있어요.

6 responsible / also teaches them / team members / school / to be

____

학교는 또한 그들에게 책임감 있는 팀원이 되도록 가르칩니다.

7 these skills / are important / 80% of employers think / a survey shows that

____

한 설문조사가 보여주길 고용주의 80%가 이런 기술들이 중요하다고 생각한다고 한다.

8 students / that's why / to school / should go

____

그렇기 때문에 학생들은 학교에 가야 한답니다.

← Step 2는 앞 쪽의 기사를 보고 답을 맞춰 보세요.

정리하기 Choose words from the box and complete the organizer.

- responsibility
- important
- solve
- practice
- jobs
- well

Main Idea Students go to school to learn how to work _________ with others.

Details

1. They can ________ teamwork and social skills in group settings.

2. School also teaches them ____________________.

3. These skills help them get _________ in the future.

Conclusion That's why students should go to school to learn these __________ skills.

✴ responsibility 책임   solve 해결하다

STEP 04

토론하기 Choose and circle the correct answers.

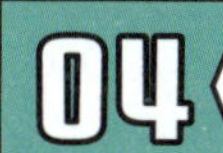

Word Bank

billion 10억

worldwide 전 세계적으로

in-game 게임 안에서의

Roblox 로블록스 (게임 이름)

Robux 로벅스 (로블록스 안에서 쓰는 게임 머니)

Minecraft 마인크래프트 (게임 이름)

own 자체의, 고유한

item 아이템

player 게임하는 사람

difference 차이점

Game Money Is for Games Only!

Over 3 billion people play video games worldwide. About 80% of popular games use their own kind of money. This money is called in-game money.

For example, Roblox uses money called Robux. Some Minecraft games make their own coins. People use game money to buy items in the game. But they cannot use it outside the game. So it's important for players to understand the difference.

⭐ 한국소비자원에 따르면, 10대 청소년 중 일부는 게임 아이템에 한 달에 10만 원 이상을 쓰기도 해요. 그래서 요즘은 학교에서도 게임 소비에 대한 교육이 필요하다는 목소리가 나오고 있어요. 게임 머니를 쓸 때 스스로 어떤 기준을 세우면 좋을까요?

1 Fill in the blanks with the correct words from the box. One word will not be used.

> o money   o buy   o in-game   o real

1 Some games have their own kind of ____________.

2 ________________ money is only used inside the game.

3 It is important to know that game money is not the same as ________ money.

2 After reading the article, circle **T**(true) or **F**(false).

1 All video games use in-game money.   T F

2 Roblox and Minecraft are examples of games that use in-game money.   T F

3 Complete the main idea sentence with words from the box.

> o outside   o own   o Robux   o game

Some games use their ________ type of money, and players can use it only inside the ____________.

1 play / worldwide / video games / over 3 billion people

____

전 세계적으로 30억 명이 넘는 사람들이 비디오 게임을 해요.

2 popular games / about 80% of / their own kind of money / use

____

약 80%의 인기 있는 게임들은 그들만의 종류의 돈을 사용합니다.

3 in-game money / is called / this money

____

이 돈은 '인게임 머니'라고 불려요.

4 Roblox / money called Robux / for example, / uses

____

예를 들어, 로블록스는 '로벅스'라는 돈을 사용해요.

5 their own coins / make / some Minecraft games

____

일부 마인크래프트 게임들은 그들만의 코인을 만들어요.

6 use / people / game money / in the game / to buy items

____

사람들은 게임 속에 있는 아이템을 사기 위해 게임 머니를 사용합니다.

7 they / outside the game / cannot use it / but

____

하지만 그들은 그것을 게임 밖에서는 사용할 수 없습니다.

8 the difference / so / to understand / it's important / for players

____

그래서 그 차이를 이해하는 것이 게임하는 사람들에게 중요해요.

← Step 2는 앞 쪽의 기사를 보고 답을 맞춰 보세요.

정리하기 Choose words from the box and complete the organizer.

- same
- outside
- inside
- popular
- games
- difference

Main Idea In-game money is used only _____________ the game.

Details

1. In-game money is common in __________ games.
2. People use it to buy items in ________.
3. This type of money cannot be used __________ the game.

Conclusion Real-life money and game money are not the ________.

❋ common 흔한

토론하기 Choose and circle the correct answers.

Do you agree with the **Main Idea**?

Word Bank

focus 집중하다

usually 보통

harmful 해로운

study 연구

shorten 짧게 만들다

attention span
집중할 수 있는 시간

task 일, 활동

Short Videos, Short Focus

A survey says over 50% of kids watch short videos every day. These videos are usually under

one minute long. They are fast, fun, and sometimes help kids learn quickly. But watching too many short videos can be harmful. According to a study, they shorten kids' attention spans. So longer tasks can feel harder for kids. Many kids can't focus well in school. Short videos are fun, but they can also hurt learning.

미국 스탠퍼드 대학 연구에 따르면, 짧은 영상을 자주 보는 아이들은 긴 수업이나 책 읽기에 더 빨리 지루함을 느낀다고 해요. 짧은 영상은 빠르게 정보를 줄 수 있지만, 주의 집중력을 떨어뜨릴 수도 있어요. 친구들은 재미있는 영상과 공부 사이에서 어떻게 균형을 지키고 있나요?

1 Fill in the blanks with the correct words from the box. One word will not be used.

1 A _____________ says many kids watch short videos every day.

2 Short videos are under one ___________ long.

3 These videos help kids _________ quickly.

2 After reading the article, circle **T**(true) or **F**(false).

1 Short videos are usually longer than 10 minutes.   T F

2 All kids focus better after watching short videos.   T F

3 Complete the main idea sentence with words from the box.

Watching a lot of _________ videos can shorten kids' ___________ spans.

1 over 50% of kids / a survey says / every day / watch short videos

____

한 설문 조사에 따르면 50%가 넘는 아이들이 매일 짧은 영상들을 본다고 해요.

2 under one minute long / are / usually / these videos

____

이런 영상들은 보통 1분 미만이에요.

3 are fast, fun, / they / learn quickly / and sometimes help kids

____

그것들은 빠르고, 재미있고, 그리고 때로는 아이들이 빨리 배우는 데 도움이 됩니다.

4 short videos / but / can be harmful / watching too many

____

하지만 짧은 영상을 너무 많이 보는 것은 해로울 수 있어요.

5 they / kids' attention spans / shorten / according to a study,

____

한 연구에 따르면, 그것들은 아이들의 집중할 수 있는 시간을 짧게 만듭니다.

6 for kids / longer tasks / so / can feel harder

____

그래서 더 긴 활동들이 아이들에게는 더 어렵게 느껴질 수 있어요.

7 many kids / in school / can't focus well

____

많은 아이들이 학교에서 집중을 잘 못하기도 해요.

8 are fun, / short videos / can also hurt / but they / learning

____

짧은 영상들은 재미있지만, 그것들은 학습에 해가 될 수도 있어요.

← Step 2는 앞 쪽의 기사를 보고 답을 맞춰 보세요.

 정리하기 **Choose words from the box and complete the organizer.**

- shorten
- harder
- careful
- quickly
- watching
- focus

Main Idea ________________ too many short videos is not good for kids.

Details

1 They can ____________ kids' attention spans.

2 Longer tasks can feel ____________ for kids.

3 Many kids can't ________ well at school.

Conclusion Kids should be ____________ when watching short videos.

✳ careful 조심하는

 토론하기 **Choose and circle the correct answers.**

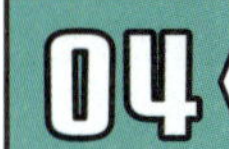

Do you agree with the **Main Idea** ?

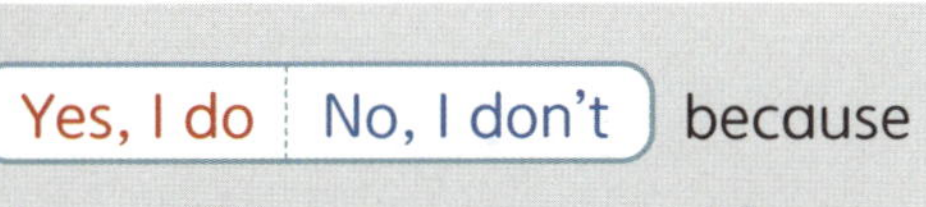

Why Do Prices Change?

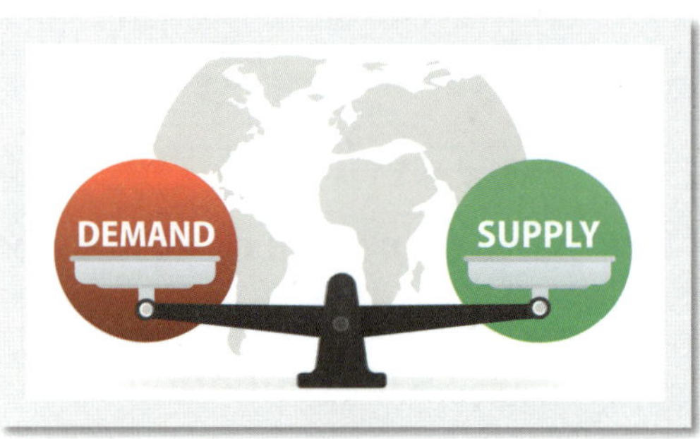

Prices are going up in many places around the world. Prices change because of supply and demand. If many people want something, the price goes up. For example, demand for ice cream goes up in summer. As a result, ice cream prices go up by about 25%. In winter, ice cream costs less because the demand is low. Businesses change prices to match supply and demand. That is why prices never stay the same.

Word Bank

supply 공급

demand 수요

as a result 그 결과로

business 기업

match 맞추다

⭐ 2021년에는 전 세계적으로 차량용 반도체가 부족해서 자동차 가격이 크게 올랐어요. 이런 현상은 '공급이 줄고 수요는 그대로일 때 가격이 오른다'는 원리를 잘 보여줘요. 수요와 공급은 우리 생활 속 가격에 큰 영향을 줘요. 친구들은 이런 원리를 가장 잘 느껴본 적이 언제인가요?

1 Fill in the blanks with the correct words from the box. One word will not be used.

> ○ down   ○ businesses   ○ price   ○ up

1 When many people want something, the ____________ goes up.

2 In summer, the price of ice cream goes ________.

3 ________________ change prices to match supply and demand.

2 After reading the article, circle **T**(true) or **F**(false).

1 Prices stay the same all the time.   T   F

2 Ice cream costs more in summer because demand is high.   T   F

3 Complete the main idea sentence with words from the box.

> ○ money   ○ prices   ○ supply   ○ world

____________ go up and down because of ____________ and demand.

기사 쓰기 Unscramble the sentences below.

1 are going up / around the world / in many places / prices

전 세계 여러 곳에서 가격들이 오르고 있어요.

2 change / prices / supply and demand / because of

가격은 공급과 수요 때문에 변해요.

3 the price / want something, / if / many people / goes up

만약 많은 사람들이 어떤 것을 원하면, 그 가격은 올라가요.

4 goes up / demand / in summer / for ice cream / for example,

예를 들어, 여름에는 아이스크림에 대한 수요가 올라갑니다.

5 ice cream prices / by about 25% / go up / as a result,

그 결과로, 아이스크림 가격은 약 25% 올라갑니다.

6 ice cream / because the demand / costs less / in winter, / is low

겨울에는, 수요가 적기 때문에 아이스크림을 사는 데 돈이 덜 들어요.

7 change / businesses / prices / supply and demand / to match

기업들은 공급과 수요에 맞추기 위해 가격을 바꿔요.

8 prices / that is why / stay the same / never

그렇기 때문에 가격은 절대로 똑같이 머물러 있지 않아요.

← Step 2는 앞 쪽의 기사를 보고 답을 맞춰 보세요.

STEP 03 — 정리하기 Choose words from the box and complete the organizer.

- control
- demand
- expensive
- supply
- more
- cheaper

Main Idea Prices change because of supply and __________.

Details

1. When __________ people want something, price goes up.
2. In summer, ice cream is more __________ because demand goes up.
3. In winter, ice cream is __________ because demand goes down.

Conclusion Supply and demand __________ prices.

※ control 조절하다

STEP 04 — 토론하기 Choose and circle the correct answers.

Do you agree with the **Main Idea**?

※ government 정부   oil 기름   whenever 언제든지

E-Scooter Out, Safety In!

Word Bank

e-scooter
전동 킥보드

accident 사고

in response
이에 대응하여

ban 금지하다

Banpo *hagwon* districts
반포 학원가

school zone
학교 주변 구역, 스쿨존

cause ~을 일으키다

fine 벌금

In 2023, over 2,000 e-scooter (electric scooter) accidents happened in Korea. In response, Seoul began banning e-scooters in some areas this March. These areas include Banpo *hagwon* districts and school zones. Many students walk there every day. The roads are small and very busy. But e-scooters can move quickly and cause accidents. If people use e-scooters in these areas, they may get a fine. This rule helps students walk more safely.

⭐ 2023년에는 전국적으로 전동 킥보드 사고가 2,000건 넘게 발생했고, 이 중 일부는 학생과 관련된 사고였어요. 그래서 서울시는 2025년 3월부터 학원가나 스쿨존처럼 사람이 많은 곳에서 전동 킥보드 이용을 제한하기 시작했어요. 친구들은 학교 주변에서 전동 킥보드를 자주 본 적이 있나요? 이런 규칙이 필요하다고 생각하나요?

1 Fill in the blanks with the correct words from the box. One word will not be used.

> o areas　　o students　　o fine　　o accidents

(1) Over 2,000 e-scooter ________________ happened in Korea in 2023.

(2) Seoul banned e-scooters in some ________ like school zones.

(3) If people ride there, they may get a ________.

2 After reading the article, circle **T**(true) or **F**(false).

(1) E-scooters are now banned in some areas in Seoul.　　T　F

(2) The new rule helps students walk more safely.　　T　F

3 Complete the main idea sentence with words from the box.

> o students　　o adults　　o e-scooter　　o rule

Seoul made a new ________ to ban e-scooters in some areas to keep ________ safe.

1 over 2,000 e-scooter accidents / in 2023, / in Korea / happened

____

2023년에, 한국에서는 2,000건이 넘는 전동 킥보드 사고가 발생했어요.

2 Seoul began / banning e-scooters / this March / in some areas / in response,

____

그 결과, 서울은 올해 3월에 몇몇 지역에서 전동 킥보드를 금지하기 시작했어요.

3 include / these areas / and school zones / Banpo *hagwon* districts

____

이 지역들에는 반포 학원가와 학교 주변 구역이 포함됩니다.

4 walk there / many students / every day

____

많은 학생들이 매일 그곳을 걸어다녀요.

5 are / and very busy / small / the roads

____

그 길들은 좁고 매우 혼잡합니다.

6 and cause / e-scooters / but / can move quickly / accidents

____

하지만 전동 킥보드는 빠르게 움직일 수 있고 사고를 일으킬 수 있어요.

7 use e-scooters / they / in these areas, / may get a fine / if people

____

만약 사람들이 이런 지역에서 전동 킥보드를 이용하면, 그들은 벌금을 받을 수도 있어요.

8 helps / this rule / walk more safely / students

____

이 규칙은 학생들이 더 안전하게 걸어다닐 수 있도록 도와줘요.

← Step 2는 앞 쪽의 기사를 보고 답을 맞춰 보세요.

- use
- accidents
- banning
- fine
- safely
- many

Main Idea Seoul is ______________ e-scooters in some areas.

Details

1. ________ students walk in these areas.

2. E-scooters can move quickly and cause ______________.

3. With this new rule, people may get a fine if they __________ e-scooters there.

Conclusion This new rule helps students walk __________.

STEP 04 토론하기 Choose and circle the correct answers.

Do you agree with the **Main Idea**?

Need Money to Make Coins!

It's not cheap to make small coins anymore. Coins are made with different metals, which cost money. A 10-won coin costs about 20 won. That's more than the coin's value! In 2023, metal prices went up by 15%. So making coins became more expensive that year. Coins are small, but they cost a lot to make. With costs rising, will we still use coins in the future?

Word Bank

coin 동전

metal 금속

value 가치

expensive 비싼

rise 오르다

⭐ 미국에서는 1센트 동전을 만드는 데 약 3.07센트가 들어, 동전 하나를 만들 때마다 손해를 보고 있어요. 이러한 이유로 미국 정부는 1센트 동전의 생산 중단 여부에 대한 논의를 진행 중이에요.(2025년 4월 기준) 친구들은 우리나라에서도 작은 단위의 동전을 없애는 것에 대해 어떻게 생각하나요?

1 Fill in the blanks with the correct words from the box. One word will not be used.

① It __________ money to make small coins.

② It is not ____________ to make coins anymore.

③ Coins are made with different kinds of ____________.

2 After reading the article, circle **T**(true) or **F**(false).

① A 10-won coin costs about 3 won to make.   T   F

② Coins were cheaper to make in 2023.   T   F

3 Complete the main idea sentence with words from the box.

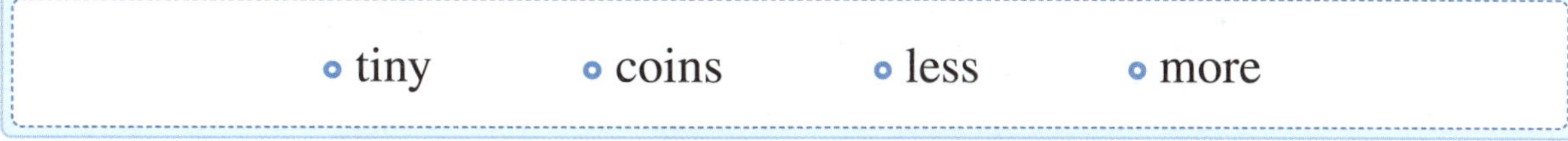

It's not cheap to make __________, and some small coins cost __________ than they are worth.

※ worth ~의 가치가 있는

기사 쓰기 Unscramble the sentences below.

1 to make / anymore / small coins / it's not cheap

작은 동전들을 만드는 것이 더 이상 저렴하지 않아요.

2 with different metals, / are made / coins / which cost money

동전들은 여러 가지 금속들로 만들어지는데, 이 금속들은 돈이 들어요.

3 about 20 won / costs / a 10-won coin

10원짜리 동전 하나는 약 20원이 듭니다.

4 the coin's value! / more than / that's

그것은 그 동전의 가치보다 비쌉니다!

5 metal prices / in 2023, / by 15% / went up

2023년에는, 금속 가격이 15% 올랐습니다.

6 became more expensive / making coins / so / that year

그래서 그 해에는 동전을 만드는 것이 더 비싸졌습니다.

7 a lot to make / but they / coins / cost / are small,

동전들은 작지만, 그것들은 만드는 데 많은 돈이 듭니다.

8 we / will / in the future? / still use coins / with costs rising,

비용이 계속 오르는데, 미래에도 우리는 동전을 여전히 쓰게 될까요?

← Step 2는 앞 쪽의 기사를 보고 답을 맞춰 보세요.

- bill
- coins
- cheap
- metals
- expensive
- costs

Main Idea It's not cheap to make __________ today.

Details
1 Coins are made with __________, which cost money.
2 These days, a 10-won coin now __________ about 20 won.
3 Small coins are no longer __________ to make.

Conclusion The cost of making coins has become more __________.

✻ bill 지폐

Do you agree with the **Main Idea**?

✻ solve 해결하다   material 재료   go up 오르다

Word Bank

MBTI
(Myers–Briggs Type Indicator의 약자)
마이어스-브릭스
유형 지표

popular 인기 있는

personality 성격

type 유형

study 연구

especially 특히

MBTI Changes As You Grow!

The MBTI is popular with kids these days. It is a test that helps them understand their personality. It also helps them understand their friends. However, MBTI types often change as they grow. According to a study, about 40% of people change their MBTI type after five years. MBTI types can change a lot, especially for children. The reason is that children change a lot as they grow. The MBTI is fun, but it may not stay the same.

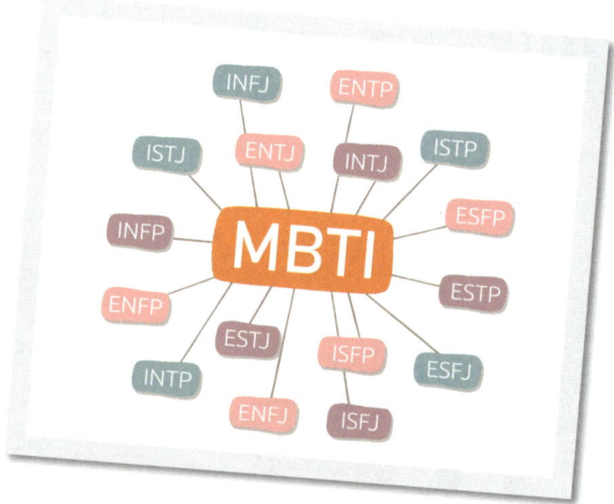

🌟 MBTI는 사람의 성격을 16가지 유형으로 나누어, 내가 어떤 성격을 가졌는지 알아보는 검사예요. 일부 친구들은 "나는 I라서 발표 못 해요." 하고 자기 성격을 딱 정해 버리는 경우도 있어요. 하지만 MBTI는 사람의 일부분을 보여 주는 도구일 뿐이고, 과학적으로 완벽한 성격 검사는 아니에요. 특히 어린이는 성격이 자주 바뀌기 때문에 결과를 너무 믿으면 안 돼요. MBTI 말고, 친구들 스스로 생각하는 자신의 성격과 장점은 무엇인가요?

1 Fill in the blanks with the correct words from the box. One word will not be used.

> • change • grow • test • understand

(1) The MBTI is a __________ that shows your personality.

(2) MBTI types often ____________ as they get older.

(3) The MBTI can help kids ______________ their friends better.

2 After reading the article, circle T(true) or F(false).

(1) The MBTI test is popular with kids today. T F

(2) Kids should never use the MBTI test. T F

3 Complete the main idea sentence with words from the box.

> • younger • children • stay • older

______________ change as they get __________, so their MBTI types may change, too.

1 is popular / the MBTI / these days / with kids

____

요즘 아이들 사이에서 MBTI가 유행이에요.

2 that helps them / their personality / understand / it is a test

____

이것은 그들이 그들의 성격을 이해하는 데 도움을 주는 테스트예요.

3 also helps them / it / their friends / understand

____

이것은 또한 그들의 친구들을 이해하는 데도 도움이 됩니다.

4 often change / as they grow / MBTI types / however,

____

하지만, 그들이 자라면서 MBTI 유형들은 자주 바뀌어요.

5 change / about 40% of people / after five years / their MBTI type

According to study, _______________________________

한 조사에 따르면, 약 40%의 사람들이 5년 후에 그들의 MBTI 유형이 바뀌었다고 해요.

6 especially / can change a lot, / for children / MBTI types

____

특히 아이들의 경우, MBTI 유형이 많이 바뀔 수 있어요.

7 as they grow / children / the reason is that / change a lot

____

그 이유는 아이들은 자라면서 많이 변하기 때문이에요.

8 is fun, / the MBTI / but / the same / it may not stay

____

MBTI는 재미있지만, 그대로 유지되지 않을 수도 있어요.

← Step 2는 앞 쪽의 기사를 보고 답을 맞춰 보세요.

정리하기 Choose words from the box and complete the organizer.

- time
- change
- different
- personality
- same
- fixed

 **Main Idea** MBTI types don't always stay the __________.

 **Details**

1. The MBTI is a test that helps kids learn about their __________.
2. But MBTI types can change with __________ for many people.
3. Kids change a lot as they grow, so their types may __________ even more.

Conclusion Kids should know that their MBTI type is not __________.

※ fixed 고정된 with time 시간이 지나면서

토론하기 Choose and circle the correct answers.

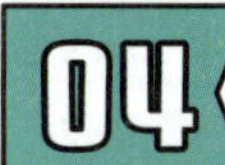

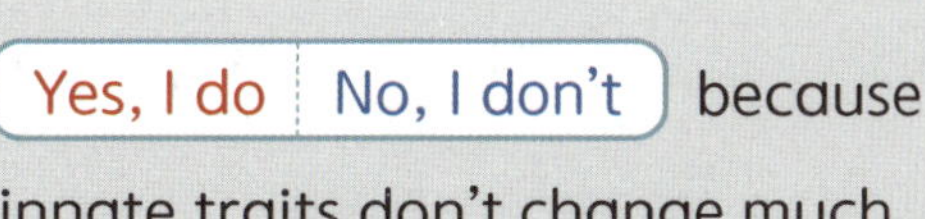

※ innate trait 타고난 성향

Word Bank

UBI 보편적 기본소득
(국가에서 모두에게 주는 돈)

take (more) jobs
(더 많은) 일자리를 차지하다

lose 잃다

Finland 핀란드

report 보고하다

lazy 게으른

UBI: Money Without Work?

Robots and AI are taking more jobs today. So many people may lose their jobs in the future. Universal basic income, or UBI, is one idea that may help. UBI gives money to all people without them needing to work. In Finland, 2,000 people got UBI for two years. They reported that they felt happier and tried more new things in their lives. But some worry that UBI makes people too lazy to work. UBI can help many people, but not everyone agrees.

⭐ 독일에서는 122명의 참가자에게 3년 동안 매달 1,200유로를 지급하는 실험을 했어요. 참가자들은 평균적으로 더 행복하고, 스트레스가 줄었고, 수면의 질이 향상되었다고 보고했어요. 흥미롭게도, 이들은 일하는 시간을 줄이지 않았고, 일부는 새로운 직업에 도전하기도 했어요. 친구들이라면 기본소득을 받으면 무엇을 해보고 싶나요?

1 Fill in the blanks with the correct words from the box. One word will not be used.

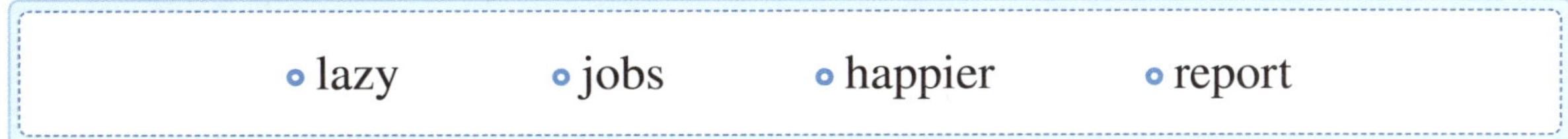

(1) Robots and AI may take more __________ in the future.

(2) Some people say UBI helps people feel __________.

(3) Others think UBI can make people too __________ to work.

2 After reading the article, circle **T**(true) or **F**(false).

(1) UBI gives money to all people even if they don't have jobs.　　T　F

(2) In Finland, 2,000 people got UBI for twenty years.　　T　F

3 Complete the main idea sentence with words from the box.

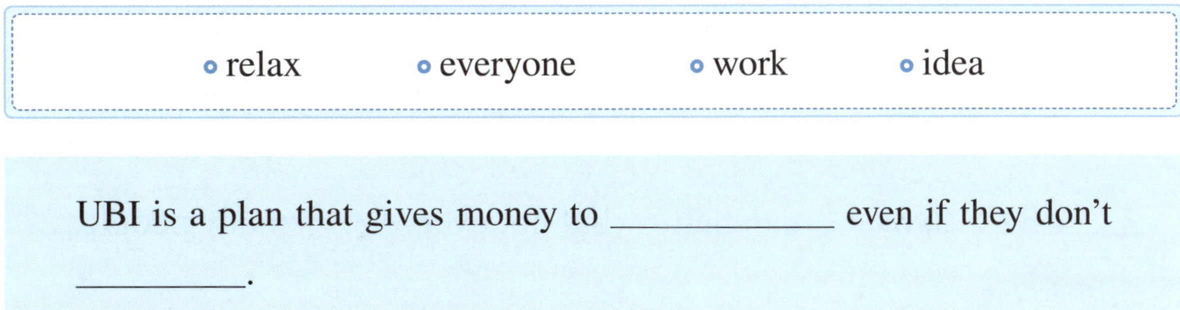

UBI is a plan that gives money to __________ even if they don't __________.

1 are taking / robots and AI / today / more jobs

____

요즘 로봇과 AI가 더 많은 일자리를 차지하고 있어요.

2 in the future / may lose / many people / so / their jobs

____

그래서 많은 사람들이 미래에 그들의 직업을 잃을 수도 있어요.

3 is one idea / universal basic income, / that may help / or UBI,

____

이를 돕기 위한 하나의 아이디어가 보편적 기본소득, 즉 UBI예요.

4 to all people / needing to work / without them / UBI gives money

____

UBI는 일할 필요 없이 모든 사람들에게 돈을 줍니다.

5 got UBI / 2,000 people / for two years / in Finland,

____

핀란드에서는, 2,000명이 2년 동안 UBI를 받았어요.

6 felt happier / in their lives / more new things / and tried / they

They reported that ____

그들이 보고하길, 그들은 더 행복하다고 느꼈고, 그들의 삶에서 더 많은 새로운 것들을 시도했다고 해요.

7 UBI makes people / that / but some worry / too lazy to work

____

하지만 어떤 사람들은 UBI가 사람들을 너무 게으르게 만들어 일을 안 하게 될까 걱정합니다.

8 UBI / agrees / can help / but not everyone / many people,

____

UBI는 많은 사람들을 도울 수 있지만, 모두가 찬성하는 건 아니에요.

← Step 2는 앞 쪽의 기사를 보고 답을 맞춰 보세요.

정리하기 Choose words from the box and complete the organizer.

- technologies
- money
- disagree
- UBI
- working
- playing

Main Idea ___________ is a new idea for the future.

Details

1. Many people might lose their jobs to _______________ like robots and AI.

2. UBI gives _______ to everyone without them needing to work.

3. Some say UBI is helpful, but others worry that people may stop ___________.

Conclusion UBI may be a good idea, but some people ____________.

STEP

04

토론하기 Choose and circle the correct answers.

Do you agree with the **Main Idea**?

Korea Needs More Kids!

In 2024, Korea had the world's lowest birth rate. More people are getting older, and fewer babies are being born. Korea is now called an aging society. In response, the government is trying hard to solve this problem. Some cities help families with babies pay rent. Others give free health care to babies. Even with this help, the birth rate remains low. Bigger changes are needed to make a real difference.

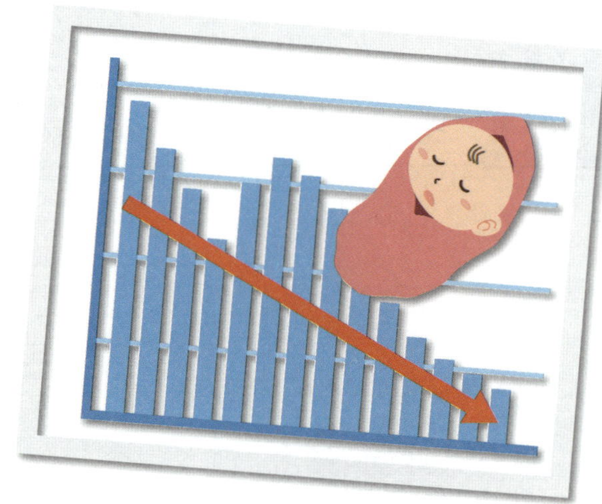

Word Bank

birth rate 출생률

aging society 고령화 사회

in response 이에 대응하여

government 정부

solve 해결하다

rent 집세

health care 의료 서비스

even with ~에도 불구하고

✪ 2024년 한국의 합계출산율은 0.72명으로, 전 세계에서 가장 낮았어요. 이는 OECD 평균인 약 1.5명의 절반도 안 되는 수준이에요. 어떤 지자체는 아이를 낳으면 최대 1,000만 원의 출산지원금을 주기도 하지만 이런 지원만으로는 충분하지 않다는 의견이 많아요. 친구들은 출산율을 높이는 방법이 어떤 것이 있다고 생각하나요?

1 Fill in the blanks with the correct words from the box. One word will not be used.

> • aging society • babies • health care • families

(1) In Korea, fewer ____________ are being born.

(2) Korea has become an ____________________.

(3) Some cities give free ____________________ to babies.

2 After reading the article, circle **T**(true) or **F**(false).

(1) Korea had the highest birth rate in 2024. T F

(2) The government is doing nothing about the low birth rate. T F

3 Complete the main idea sentence with words from the box.

> • changes • birthday • rent • birth rate

Korea's ____________________ is the lowest in the world, and big ____________ are needed to fix the problem.

1 had / Korea / the world's / in 2024, / lowest birth rate

____

2024년에, 한국은 세계에서 가장 낮은 출생률을 가지고 있었어요.

2 are getting older, / more people / are being born / and fewer babies

____

더 많은 사람들이 나이가 들어가고 있고, 더 적은 수의 아기들이 태어나고 있어요.

3 an aging society / is now called / Korea

____

한국은 이제 고령화 사회라고 불립니다.

4 is trying hard / to solve / the government / this problem / in response,

____

그 결과, 정부는 이 문제를 해결하기 위해 열심히 노력하고 있어요.

5 help / pay rent / some cities / families with babies

____

어떤 도시들은 아기들이 있는 가족들이 집세를 내는 걸 도와줘요.

6 free health care / others / give / to babies

____

다른 곳들(다른 도시들)은 아기들에게 무료 의료 서비스를 제공해요.

7 the birth rate / remains low / even with this help,

____

이런 도움에도 불구하고, 출생률은 여전히 낮게 유지됩니다.

8 are needed / bigger changes / a real difference / to make

____

진정한 변화를 만들기 위해서는 더 큰 변화가 필요해요.

← Step 2는 앞 쪽의 기사를 보고 답을 맞춰 보세요.

- lowest
- older
- solve
- children
- younger
- raise

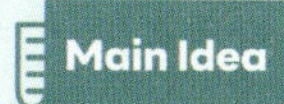
Main Idea Korea has the __________ birth rate.

Details

1. Fewer families are having ______________.

2. Korea is becoming an aging society because the population is getting __________.

3. So the government is trying hard to ________ the problem.

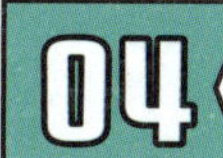
Conclusion However, big changes are needed to ________ the birth rate.

※ raise 증가시키다   population 인구

STEP 04 토론하기 **Choose and circle the correct answers.**

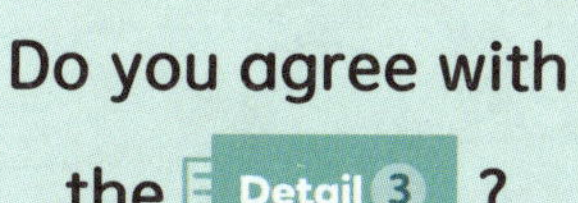

The Sharing Economy: Smart or Risky?

More people want to use things without buying them. The sharing economy lets people borrow cars, bikes, and homes. In 2023, over 30% of Koreans used sharing services. Sharing helps people save money and reduce waste. But some people worry about safety and trust. Shared homes can feel unsafe to some people. Shared bikes sometimes get lost or broken easily. Yet the sharing economy keeps growing worldwide.

Word Bank

sharing economy 공유 경제

risky 위험한

let ~하게 하다

safety 안전

trust 신뢰

unsafe 안전하지 않은

get lost 분실되다

yet 그럼에도 불구하고

⭐ 2023년 조사에 따르면, 한국에서 가장 많이 이용된 공유 서비스는 배달앱과 공유 킥보드였어요. 특히 10대와 20대는 공유 자전거나 공유 킥보드를 자주 이용한다고 해요. 하지만 이용하는 사람이 많다 보니, 기기가 망가지거나 안전 장비가 빠진 경우도 자주 생긴대요. 친구들은 이런 공유 물건들을 더 안전하게 사용하려면 어떤 노력이 필요하다고 생각하나요?

1 Fill in the blanks with the correct words from the box. One word will not be used.

> ○ bikes   ○ safety   ○ money   ○ sharing

(1) The _________ economy helps people borrow things like cars and homes.

(2) Sharing services can help people save ___________.

(3) Some people worry about ___________ when using shared homes.

2 After reading the article, circle **T**(true) or **F**(false).

(1) In 2023, only 3% of Koreans used the sharing economy.   T   F

(2) Some shared bikes can get broken or lost.   T   F

3 Complete the main idea sentence with words from the box.

> ○ spend   ○ waste   ○ save   ○ borrow

The sharing economy lets people ___________ things instead of buying them, so people can _________ money.

1 want to use things / more people / buying them / without

____

더 많은 사람들이 물건들을 사지 않고도 사용하길 원해요.

2 borrow / lets people / cars, bikes, and homes / the sharing economy

____

공유 경제는 사람들이 자동차, 자전거, 집을 빌릴 수 있게 해줘요.

3 over 30% of Koreans / in 2023, / sharing services / used

____

2023년에는, 한국인의 30% 이상이 공유 서비스를 이용했습니다.

4 helps people / save money / reduce waste / and / sharing

____

공유하는 것은 돈을 아끼고, 쓰레기를 줄이는 데 도움됩니다.

5 worry about / some people / safety and trust / but

____

하지만 어떤 사람들은 안전과 신뢰에 대해 걱정해요.

6 unsafe / can feel / to some people / shared homes

____

어떤 사람들에게는 공유하는 집은 안전하지 않게 느껴질 수 있어요.

7 broken easily / sometimes get lost / shared bikes / or

____

공유 자전거는 때때로 분실되거나 쉽게 고장 나기도 해요.

8 the sharing economy / yet / worldwide / keeps growing

____

그럼에도 불구하고 공유 경제는 전 세계적으로 계속 성장하고 있어요.

← Step 2는 앞 쪽의 기사를 보고 답을 맞춰 보세요.

- useful
- shopping
- buying
- worry
- economy
- waste

Main Idea The sharing ___________ is becoming popular around the world.

Details
1. The sharing economy helps people borrow things instead of __________ them.
2. It helps people save money and reduce ___________.
3. But some people ___________ about safety and trust when using shared things.

Conclusion Sharing services are ___________, but they have some problems.

STEP

04 토론하기 Choose and circle the correct answers.

Do you agree with the **Detail ①** ?

※ comfortable 편한

Words Online Matter, Too!

음원 듣기

Word Bank

online 온라인에서

matter 중요하다

comment 댓글, 의견

Internet 인터넷

mean 심한, 못된

break the law 법을 어기다

jail 감옥

bullying 괴롭힘

careful 조심하는

real life 현실

Bad comments online are now a big problem. The Internet helps people talk and share ideas easily. But some words can make others feel sad or hurt. In 2023, about 15% of students felt sad because of bad comments. Mean words and lies online can also break the law in Korea. Some people have gone to jail for online bullying. We must be careful with our words online. Words online are as important as words in real life.

⭐ 많은 SNS 플랫폼들이 악성 댓글을 자동으로 감지하고, 사용자에게 경고 메시지를 보내는 기능을 도입했어요. 이러한 기능은 사용자들이 나쁜 말을 쓰기 전에 다시 한번 생각하게 도와줘요. 친구들은 이런 기능이 온라인에서의 예절을 지키는 데 도움이 된다고 생각하나요?

1 Fill in the blanks with the correct words from the box. One word will not be used.

> ○ careful　　○ mean　　○ law　　○ online

(1) Some students felt sad after reading bad things ___________.

(2) We must be ___________ with what we say online.

(3) ___________ comments on the Internet can break the law.

2 After reading the article, circle T(true) or F(false).

(1) People can share their thoughts easily on the Internet.　　T　F

(2) Some people have gone to jail because of online bullying.　　T　F

3 Complete the main idea sentence with words from the box.

> ○ English　　○ respect　　○ real-life　　○ matter

Online words ___________, just like ___________ words.

✽ respect 존중하다

1 a big problem / are now / bad comments online

____

요즘 온라인에서의 나쁜 댓글들이 큰 문제가 되고 있어요.

2 helps people / the Internet / easily / talk and share ideas

____

인터넷은 사람들이 쉽게 이야기하고 생각을 나눌 수 있도록 도와줍니다.

3 sad or hurt / some words / others feel / can make / but

____

하지만 어떤 말은 다른 사람들을 슬프게 하거나 상처받게 만들 수 있어요.

4 bad comments / because of / felt sad / about 15% of students / in 2023,

____

2023년에, 약 15%의 학생들이 나쁜 댓글들 때문에 슬펐다고 느꼈어요.

5 mean words / the law in Korea / can also break / and lies online

____

또한, 온라인에서의 심한 말이나 거짓말은 한국에서 법을 어길 수도 있어요.

6 for online bullying / some people / have gone to jail

____

어떤 사람들은 온라인 괴롭힘 때문에 감옥에 갔어요.

7 we / our words online / with / must be careful

____

우리는 온라인에서의 말에 신중해야 해요.

8 are as important as / words online / in real life / words

____

온라인에서의 말도 현실에서의 말처럼 중요해요.

← Step 2는 앞 쪽의 기사를 보고 답을 맞춰 보세요.

정리하기 Choose words from the box and complete the organizer.

- break
- careful
- comment
- hurt
- Internet
- serious

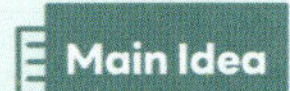 **Main Idea** What we say online is just as ___________ as in real life.

 **Details**

1 It is easy to talk and share ideas on the _______________.

2 But mean online comments _________ others.

3 Some mean comments can also _________ the law.

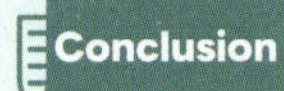 **Conclusion** That's why we should be ___________ before we make comments online.

※ serious 심각한, 중대한

토론하기 Choose and circle the correct answers.

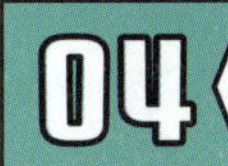

Do you agree with the **Main Idea** ?

※ face to face 직접, 마주 보고

bank account 은행 계좌

save 저축하다

interest (rate) 이자(율)

extra 추가의

amount 양, 금액

around 약, ~쯤

little by little 조금씩

plan 계획

goal 목표

Put It in the Bank; Watch It Grow!

Many children today use bank accounts to save their money. They put money in banks to keep it safe and to help it grow. Banks give interest, which is a small extra amount of money. In 2024, interest rates in Korea were around 3%. Interest helps money grow little by little. Banks also help kids with money plans and saving goals. That's why saving in a bank is the first step for many kids. It's one smart way to learn about saving and growing money.

⭐ 2024년 한국의 은행 이자율은 약 3%였어요. 1만 원을 1년 동안 은행에 넣어두면, 약 300원이 더 생기는 셈이에요. 어떤 친구는 책을 사기 위해 용돈을 조금씩 모아서 통장에 저축하고 있어요. 친구들은 어떤 목표를 위해 돈을 모아본 적 있나요?

1 Fill in the blanks with the correct words from the box. One word will not be used.

(1) Children put money in the __________ to keep it safe.

(2) Banks give interest, which is ____________ money.

(3) The money can __________ little by little with time.

2 After reading the article, circle **T**(true) or **F**(false).

(1) Many children use bank accounts to save money.　　T　F

(2) Interest means kids get extra money from saving.　　T　F

3 Complete the main idea sentence with words from the box.

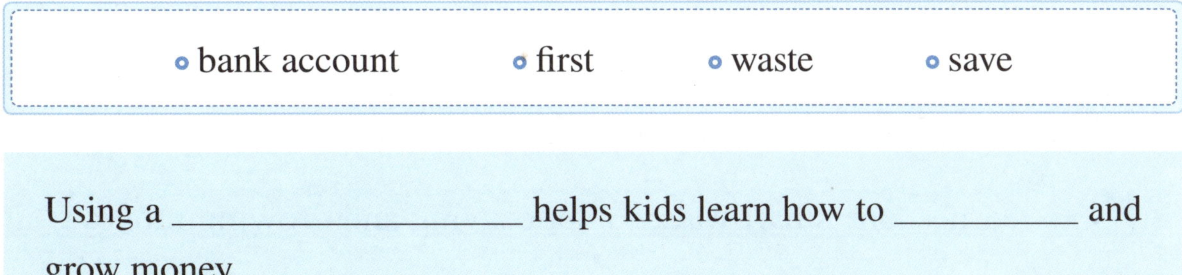

Using a ___________________ helps kids learn how to ____________ and grow money.

1 their money / use bank accounts / to save / many children today

____

요즘 많은 아이들이 그들의 돈을 저축하기 위해 은행 계좌를 사용합니다.

2 put money / they / in banks / and to help it grow / to keep it safe

____

그들은 돈을 안전하게 보관하고 불리기 위해 은행에 넣어요.

3 a small extra amount of money / give interest, / banks / which is

____

은행은 이자를 주는데, 그것은 돈에 조금 더해지는 작은 금액이에요.

4 were / interest rates in Korea / around 3% / in 2024,

____

2024년에, 한국의 이자율은 약 3%였습니다.

5 helps money / interest / little by little / grow

____

이자는 돈이 조금씩 늘어나도록 도와줘요.

6 also help / with money plans and saving goals / kids / banks

____

은행은 아이들이 돈 계획과 저축 목표를 만드는 데에도 도움을 줘요.

7 saving in a bank / that's why / for many kids / is the first step

____

그렇기 때문에 많은 아이들에게 은행에 저축하는 것이 첫걸음입니다.

8 to learn / one smart way / about saving and growing money / it's

____

이것은 저축과 돈을 불리는 법을 배우는 똑똑한 방법 중 하나예요.

← Step 2는 앞 쪽의 기사를 보고 답을 맞춰 보세요.

정리하기 Choose words from the box and complete the organizer.

- goals
- interest
- safe
- first
- wise
- borrow

Main Idea A bank is a good place for kids to start learning about _________ money habits.

Details

1. Kids put their money in banks to keep it _________.

2. Banks give _________, which helps saved money slowly grow.

3. Banks also help children with money planning for future _________.

Conclusion That's why saving in a bank is the _________ step for many kids.

※ wise 현명한 borrow 빌리다

STEP 04

토론하기 Choose and circle the correct answers.

Do you agree with the **Main Idea**?

Should 16-Year-Olds Vote?

Today, most countries let 18-year-olds vote in elections. However, some countries even allow 16-year-olds to vote. Austria is one of them, and it started this rule in 2007. Some people say these younger teens care about the future. They believe they can make smart choices. Others say teens under 18 need more experience to vote well. They think the voting age should remain 18. This debate continues in many countries.

Word Bank

vote 투표하다

election 선거

even 심지어 ~도

allow 허락하다

rule 규칙

care about ~에 관심을 가지다

experience 경험

debate 논쟁, 토론

continue 계속되다

⭐ 오스트리아는 2007년부터 16살부터 투표할 수 있는 법을 만들었어요. 뉴질랜드, 브라질, 아르헨티나 같은 나라들도 16세 투표를 허용하고 있어요. 하지만 미국, 일본, 한국은 여전히 18세부터 투표할 수 있어요. 친구들은 투표 나이가 더 어려져도 괜찮다고 생각하나요? 아니면 지금처럼 유지하는 게 좋을까요?

1 Fill in the blanks with the correct words from the box. One word will not be used.

(1) Some people say 16-year-olds can also _________ well.

(2) They believe these younger teens _________ about the future.

(3) Others say the voting age should _________ 18.

2 After reading the article, circle **T**(true) or **F**(false).

(1) Most countries let 18-year-olds vote.   T F

(2) Austria allows teens to vote at 14.   T F

3 Complete the main idea sentence with words from the box.

parents   teens   law   choices

Some people think younger _________ can make good _________ when they vote.

 기사 쓰기 Unscramble the sentences below.

1 let / most countries / vote in elections / 18-year-olds / today,

____

오늘날, 대부분의 나라들은 18세가 된 사람들이 선거에서 투표하도록 허용해요.

2 some countries / however, / 16-year-olds to vote / even allow

____

하지만, 일부 나라들은 심지어 16세 청소년들이 투표하는 것도 허용해요.

3 is one of them, / in 2007 / started this rule / Austria / and it

____

오스트리아가 그 중 하나이고, 그것(오스트리아)은 2007년에 이 규칙을 시작했습니다.

4 these younger teens / some people say / the future / care about

____

어떤 사람들은 이 어린 청소년들이 미래를 중요하게 생각한다고 말합니다.

5 smart choices / they / they believe / can make

____

그들은 그들(청소년들)이 현명한 선택을 할 수 있다고 믿어요.

6 teens under 18 / others say / need / to vote well / more experience

____

다른 사람들은 18세 미만의 청소년들이 투표를 잘하기 위해서는 더 많은 경험이 필요하다고 말해요.

7 the voting age / 18 / should remain / they think

____

그들은 투표 연령이 18세로 유지되어야 한다고 생각합니다.

8 continues / this debate / in many countries

____

이 논쟁은 많은 나라들에서 계속되고 있어요.

← Step 2는 앞 쪽의 기사를 보고 답을 맞춰 보세요.

- same
- allow
- countries
- voting age
- different
- ready

Main Idea Different countries have ____________ voting ages.

Details

1. Most countries ________ teens to vote at 18.
2. But some ___________, like Austria, let teens vote at 16.
3. Some people worry that these younger teens are not ________ to vote.

Conclusion The debate on the best _______________ continues.

※ voting age 투표 연령

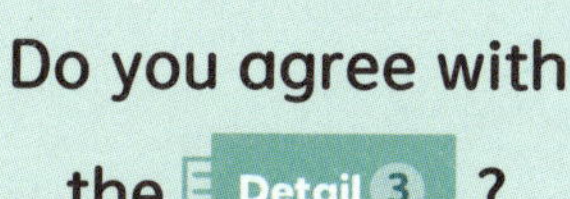

Credit Cards Are Not Free Money

Word Bank

credit card 신용카드

report 보고서

100 million 1억

use 사용하다

cash 현금

borrow 빌리다

pay back 갚다

wisely 현명하게

A report says over 100 million credit cards are used in Korea. Many people use cards to pay without cash. Cards make shopping easy, but they are not real money. It is important to remember that it is borrowed money. You must pay back the money after using a credit card. If you pay late, you pay extra money. So you must be careful not to spend too much. Cards can be helpful, but they must be used wisely.

⭐ 2024년 말, 한국의 신용카드 연체율은 1.65%로 10년 만에 최고치를 기록했어요. '연체율'은 카드값을 제때 갚지 못한 액수의 비율을 말해요. 이는 많은 사람들이 카드로 사용한 돈을 제때 갚지 못하고 있다는 뜻이에요. 친구들은 왜 사람들이 카드값을 제때 갚지 못하는 경우가 많다고 생각하나요?

1 Fill in the blanks with the correct words from the box. One word will not be used.

(1) Many people use credit cards to shop without using __________.

(2) A credit card is ______________ money that must be paid back.

(3) If you pay __________, you pay extra money.

2 After reading the article, circle **T**(true) or **F**(false).

(1) Around 100 credit cards are used in Korea now.　　T　F

(2) Borrowed money is the same as free money.　　T　F

3 Complete the main idea sentence with words from the box.

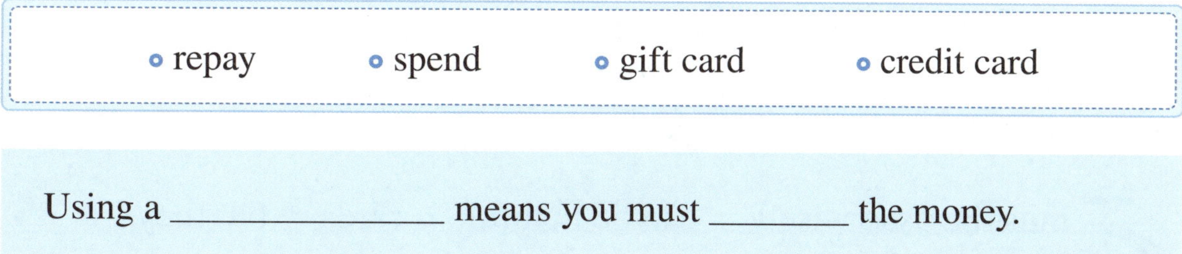

※ repay (빌린 돈을) 갚다

119

기사 쓰기 Unscramble the sentences below.

1 over 100 million credit cards / a report says / in Korea / are used

____

한 보고서에 따르면 한국에서 1억 장이 넘는 신용카드가 사용되고 있다고 해요.

2 without cash / use cards / many people / to pay

____

많은 사람들이 현금 없이 결제하기 위해 카드를 사용해요.

3 make shopping easy, / cards / but they / real money / are not

____

카드는 쇼핑을 쉽게 만들어 주지만, 그것들은 실제 돈은 아니에요.

4 borrowed money / to remember / it is important / that it is

____

그것이 빌린 돈이라는 것을 기억하는 것이 중요해요.

5 a credit card / must pay back / you / after using / the money

____

신용카드를 사용한 후에는 그 돈을 갚아야 합니다.

6 extra money / you / if you pay late, / pay

____

만약 늦게 갚으면, 추가적인 돈을 냅니다.

7 too much / not to spend / you / so / must be careful

____

그래서 당신은 너무 많이 쓰지 않도록 조심해야 합니다.

8 must be used wisely / can be helpful, / cards / but they

____

카드는 유용하지만, 현명하게 사용되어야 해요.

← Step 2는 앞 쪽의 기사를 보고 답을 맞춰 보세요.

- wisely
- pay
- free
- credit cards
- borrowed
- without

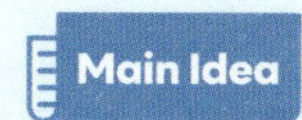 **Main Idea** _________________ are easy to use but need to be used carefully.

 **Details**

1. Credit cards let people buy things __________ using cash.
2. But the money you spend with a card is _____________.
3. That means you have to ________ back the money later.

 **Conclusion** It is important to know how credit cards work and to use them ___________.

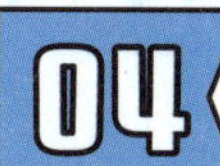

Do you agree with the **Main Idea**?

Word Bank

Mars 화성

scientist 과학자

last 지속되다

space 공간

exploration 탐사

SpaceX
스페이스엑스
(우주선을 만드는 회사)

take care of
~을 보살피다

Can Mars Be Our New Earth?

Scientists say the Earth may not last forever. They say the Earth does not have enough space, food, or water. That's why Mars explorations are getting more attention these days. Some people think Mars could be the next home for humans. Elon Musk's company, SpaceX, is working on this dream. It plans to send people to Mars one day. Others say we should help the Earth first. Should we dream about Mars or take care of the Earth instead?

✪ 2024년 기준으로 NASA와 SpaceX 등 여러 기관들이 화성 탐사 계획을 세우고 있어요. 지금까지 화성에 간 로봇 탐사선은 20개가 넘고, 과학자들은 사람이 살 수 있는지 연구 중이에요. 하지만 어떤 사람들은 지구를 먼저 살리는 게 더 중요하다고 말해요. 친구들은 미래에는 사람들이 진짜로 화성에 살게 될 수 있다고 생각하나요? 아니면 지구를 먼저 지켜야 한다고 생각하나요?

1 Fill in the blanks with the correct words from the box. One word will not be used.

> ○ Mars   ○ explorations   ○ space   ○ Earth

(1) Scientists say the ___________ will not last forever.

(2) Some say ________ may become a new home for people.

(3) People are more interested in Mars ______________ now.

2 After reading the article, circle **T**(true) or **F**(false).

(1) The Earth has more than enough food and water for the future.   **T** **F**

(2) Some say the Moon could be a new home for humans.   **T** **F**

3 Complete the main idea sentence with words from the box.

> ○ leave   ○ living   ○ protect   ○ future

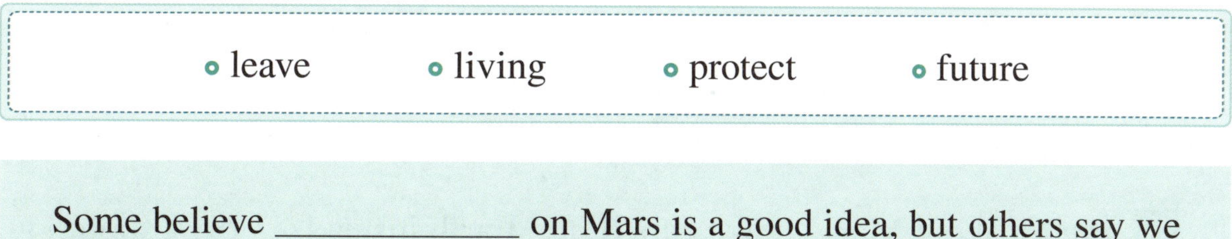

Some believe ______________ on Mars is a good idea, but others say we must ______________ the Earth first.

기사 쓰기 Unscramble the sentences below.

1 the Earth / scientists say / forever / may not last

____

과학자들은 지구가 영원히 지속되지 않을 수도 있다고 말해요.

2 enough space, food, or water / they say / does not have / the Earth

____

그들은 지구에 충분한 공간, 음식, 혹은 물이 없다고 말합니다.

3 Mars explorations / these days / more attention / are getting / that's why

____

그렇기 때문에 요즘에는 화성 탐사가 더 많은 주목을 받고 있습니다.

4 Mars could be / some people think / for humans / the next home

____

어떤 사람들은 화성이 인류의 다음 집이 될 수 있다고 생각해요.

5 SpaceX, / this dream / is working on / Elon Musk's company,

____

일론 머스크의 회사인 스페이스X는 이 꿈을 이루려고 일하고 있어요.

6 to send people / it plans / one day / to Mars

____

이곳은 언젠가 사람들을 화성으로 보내는 것을 계획하고 있어요.

7 the Earth first / we / others say / should help

____

다른 사람들은 지구를 먼저 도와야 한다고 말해요.

8 dream about Mars / take care of the Earth instead? / or / should we

____

우리는 화성을 꿈꿔야 할까요, 아니면 대신에 지구를 돌봐야 할까요?

← Step 2는 앞 쪽의 기사를 보고 답을 맞춰 보세요.

 정리하기 **Choose words from the box and complete the organizer.**

- agrees
- save
- alien
- home
- answer
- last

Main Idea Mars could be the next _________ for humans.

Details

1 Earth has many problems and may not _________ forever.

2 Some say Mars is the ___________ to the problem.

3 Others say we must _________ the Earth first.

Conclusion The dream of life on Mars is growing, but not everyone _________.

※ save 구하다 alien 외계인

 토론하기 **Choose and circle the correct answers.**

Do you agree with the **Main Idea**?

Yes, I do | No, I don't because no one has lived there before, so it's too dangerous.

Yes, I do | No, I don't because Mars is the most earthlike planet we know.

※ earthlike 지구와 비슷한 planet 행성

Word Bank

save / saving
저축하다 / 저축

invest / investing
투자하다 / 투자

future 미래

stock 주식

house 집

risk 위험

investor 투자자

Should You Save, Invest, or Both?

Many people want to grow their money for the future. Some people save money in banks. Saving is safer but grows money slowly. Other people invest their money to grow it faster. But investing, like in stocks or houses, has more risk. For example, in 2023, about 25% of investors lost money. That's why people use both saving and investing. By using both, people can grow their money without too much risk.

2023년, 20대와 30대 주식 투자자의 수가 2년 연속 줄었어요. 요즘 젊은 세대는 돈을 많이 버는 것보다, 안전하게 관리하는 걸 더 중요하게 여긴다고 해요. 그래서 투자보다는 '안정'과 '신중함'을 먼저 생각하는 사람들이 점점 늘고 있어요. 친구들은 돈을 관리할 때 어떤 방법이 가장 현명하다고 생각하나요?

1 Fill in the blanks with the correct words from the box. One word will not be used.

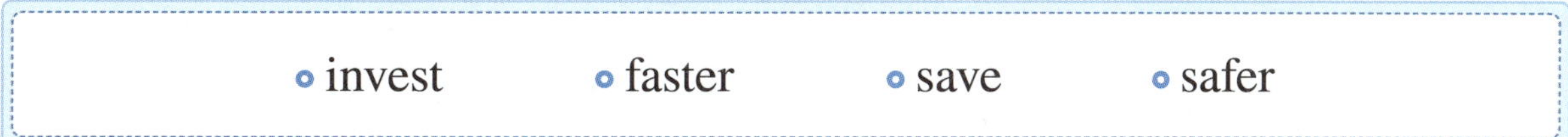

1 Some people __________ money in a bank.

2 Others __________ their money in stocks or houses.

3 Saving is __________ than investing.

2 After reading the article, circle **T**(true) or **F**(false).

1 Saving money grows your money very quickly.   T   F

2 About 25% of investors lost money in 2023.   T   F

3 Complete the main idea sentence with words from the box.

∘ spending   ∘ saving   ∘ shopping   ∘ investing

It's smart to use both __________ and __________.

기사 쓰기 Unscramble the sentences below.

1 want to grow / many people / for the future / their money

———————————————————————

많은 사람들이 미래를 위해 그들의 돈을 불리고 싶어 합니다.

2 money / save / in banks / some people

———————————————————————

어떤 사람들은 돈을 은행에 저축해요.

3 is safer / saving / but / slowly / grows money

———————————————————————

저축은 더 안전하지만 돈을 천천히 불려요.

4 faster / their money / invest / to grow it / other people

———————————————————————

다른 사람들은 그것(돈)을 더 빨리 불리기 위해 그들의 돈을 투자합니다.

5 investing, / but / like in stocks or houses, / more risk / has

———————————————————————

하지만 주식이나 집과 같은 것에 투자하는 것은 더 많은 위험을 가지고 있어요.

6 money / in 2023, / lost / about 25% of investors / for example,

———————————————————————

예를 들어, 2023년에는 약 25%의 투자자들이 돈을 잃었어요.

7 people / that's why / both saving and investing / use

———————————————————————

그렇기 때문에 사람들은 저축과 투자 둘 다 사용해요.

8 can grow their money / by using both, / people / without too much risk

———————————————————————

둘 다 함께 사용함으로써, 사람들은 너무 큰 위험 없이 돈을 불릴 수 있어요.

← Step 2는 앞 쪽의 기사를 보고 답을 맞춰 보세요.

- slowly
- both
- risk
- investing
- grow
- quickly

Main Idea Saving and investing are two ways to _________ money.

Details

1 Saving in a bank is safe, but it grows money ___________.

2 Investing can grow money faster, but it has more _________.

3 The reason is that people can lose money by ___________.

Conclusion Saving and investing are useful in different ways, so people often use _________.

STEP
04 토론하기 Choose and circle the correct answers.

Do you agree with the  **?**

MEMO

바빠 영어신문
NEWS TIMES
뉴스 타임스

Dictation

① QR코드로 받아쓰기 음원을 듣고 빈칸에 단어를 채워 보세요.
② 정답을 확인한 후, 틀린 부분만 집중해서 다시 들어 보면 최고!

내가 틀린 문제를 스스로 정리하는 습관을 들이면, 시간이 오래 흘러도 계속 기억할 수 있어요!

No More Social Media for Kids!

정답: 10쪽

Australia ______ ______ ______ kids under 16 use social media.

They ____________ ______ apps like TikTok and Instagram.

The rule ___ ____ _______ kids safe online.

Some people say social media is ______ ____ _________ ________ .

_________ think the rule is _____ _______ .

Also, this rule _____ ______ without parents' __________ .

Companies that break this law may get _____ _______ .

This new rule _____ _________ how kids use social media.

Taxes: The Price of a Better Life

People _______ ________ to help everyone.

In Korea, about 40% of tax money ____ _______ for essential services.

Taxes _______ schools and ______ teachers so children can ________ .

________ also help build hospitals and buy medicine.

Many people ___________ ____ these important places.

For example, taxes pay for ________ ______

______________ .

Without taxes, these jobs _________ ____ _______ .

That is why paying taxes ____ ____________ .

음원 듣기
정답: 18쪽

AI Is Smart, but People Teach Best

AI, or artificial intelligence, is ___ __________ ___________ system.

It ___ _______ in games, robots, online shopping, and more.

AI is also used in ____________ but cannot __________ people.

People ______________ feelings and __________ students better.

Some say AI makes learning _________ _____ ________.

However, AI _______ _____ _________ answer every question __________.

AI still needs more ______________ to teach like people.

This is ______ humans are still _____ _____ __________.

The Bitcoin Pizza Story

정답: 22쪽

Bitcoin is digital money ________ ______ online payments.

The first Bitcoin ______________ in the real world ______________ in 2010.

A man __________ two pizzas with 10,000 Bitcoin.

This was ______ ________ ________ Bitcoin was used to buy ______________.

At that time, Bitcoin was ______ ________.

Today, 1 Bitcoin is worth ________ ______ ₩100 million.

The day ____ ______ ________ Bitcoin Pizza Day.

Bitcoin __________ more popular ______ this event.

Enjoy *Mukbang*, but Stay Healthy!

정답: 26쪽

All around the _________ , *mukbang* is getting popular.

Mukbang is a video of people _________ _________ .

Some people _________ it because of the _________

_________ .

Others watch *mukbang* when they eat alone.

Mukbang _________ people feel _________ _________ .

But thousands of *mukbang* YouTubers eat a lot ____

_________ .

This can make people follow their _____________

_________ _________ .

Therefore, people should _________ *mukbang* ___________ .

Why Buy New? Shop Smart!

_________________ __________ is the new shopping trend.

Secondhand shopping means buying ______ ________.

It is __________ ______ buying new things.

It also reduces _______ and __________.

It _________ landfill waste ____ ______ ________.

In addition, secondhand stores _____ many unique items.

People ______ searching for these ________ items.

That is why secondhand shopping ___ __________ __________.

No-Kids Zones: Good or Bad?

정답: 34쪽

Kids are not ___________ in some places in Korea.

These places _____ ________ no-kids zones.

According to ___ __________ _______, there are ______ ______ no-kids zones.

Some people think this is ___ ________ ______.

They say it helps ________ enjoy ______ time.

But others think it is ________ to kids and families.

_________ also want ________ to go with their _________.

People have ____________ _________ about no-kids zones.

08 Pets Need Insurance, Too

음원 듣기

정답: 38쪽

_________ people are getting ______ every year.

They ______ their pets as _________ ___________ .

They want to ______ ______ _____ ____ their pets.

But animal hospitals can be ___________ .

Average _____ _______ can cost ₩800,000 a year per pet.

_________ , pet insurance helps _____ ______ them.

It also helps pets get ___________ quickly.

That is ______ more people _____ ___________ pet insurance.

정답: 42쪽

Will Schools Have Fewer Tests?

In Korea, students have _________ _____ at school and academies.

In a survey, _________ _____ ___ ____ _________ _________ feel stress from tests.

Too much stress is not _________ for students.

That is why some people say ________ tests are better.

_________ _________ are already trying _____ _______ to test students.

_________ and ________ can ________ exams.

_________ say this can help students _____ _______.

_____ _______ of testing may change ___ _____.

10 No Cashier? No Problem?

In __________ years, ______________ stores have been ______________.

Unmanned stores use ______________ instead of __________.

This ______ ______ for busy people.

______________ ________ also do not have to _____ workers.

____ ___________, businesses ____ ______ millions of won ______ ______.

But cashiers may ______ their jobs.

Older people may not ___________ the new technology.

Unmanned stores are ______________, but they _____ ____ ____ everyone.

Zoo: Safe Homes or Small Prisons?

음원 듣기

정답: 50쪽

Growing _________ for animals' __________ brings more _________________ to zoos.

Zoos help protect _________________ animals from harm.

Zoos help them ________ in number.

____ _________, there are ______ ______, including both _________ and __________ ones.

These zoos give kids ______ __________ to learn about animals.

But some people believe animals __________ ______ ______ in zoos.

They may not feel ______ and may get ___________.

People have ____________ __________ about zoos.

Why Do People Use *Jeonse*?

정답: 54쪽

It's getting __________ to buy a home in Korea.

One __________ ________ is *Jeonse*, a _________
housing system.

People do not have to _____ _____ every month.

_________, they ______ a lot of money at the beginning.

___________, they get their money back when they
_______ ____.

It also gives the homeowners money for ____________.

Jeonse helps both _____________ and _________.

This is ______ many people _________ *Jeonse*.

Do You Want to Be a YouTuber?

정답: 58쪽

___ _________ _________ says _______ ____% of kids want to be YouTubers.

They like _________ videos and _________ their hobbies.

Some YouTubers make ___ ____ ____ _________, too.

Top kid YouTubers make _________ of won every year.

But making videos _______ a lot of time.

Some YouTubers feel _______ ____ _________.

Cyberbullying is also ___ ____ _________ for them.

_______ why kids _________ ______ carefully _________ becoming YouTubers.

Brands: More Than Just a Name

정답: 62쪽

______________ say brand images ________ what people buy.

________ _________ help people show ______ they are.

Some people like Apple for its ________, _________ image.

Some people buy Nike for its ________, ________ image.

People ______ from brands with images they like.

This is ______ brands work hard to make _______ _________.

For example, Apple and Nike _______ trillions of won ____ ______ in 2023.

This shows ______ ___________ brand images are.

Why Do We Have to Go to School?

음원 듣기
정답: 66쪽

In the age of AI, working well with others __________ more.

____ ________, children can learn important skills like __________.

In addition to school subjects, students learn __________ ______ ________.

They ______ ___ others and ______ ideas.

Students can _________ these skills in group settings.

School also _________ them to ___ ____________ team members.

A survey shows that 80% of __________ think these skills are important.

That's why students _________ ___ ___ ________.

Game Money Is for Games Only!

___________ ___ __________ people play video games worldwide.

__________ ____% of popular games use their own kind of money.

This money ___ _________ in-game money.

For example, Roblox uses money ________ Robux.

Some Minecraft games make _______ ______ _______.

People ______ game money to buy items in the game.

But they _________ _____ it outside the game.

So ____ ___________ for players ___ ______________ the difference.

Short Videos, Short Focus

음원 듣기
정답: 74쪽

___ _________ says over 50% of kids _________ short videos every day.

These videos are usually _________ _________ _________ _________.

They are fast, fun, and sometimes help kids learn _________.

But watching _____ _______ ______ videos can be _________.

According to a study, they _________ kids' attention spans.

So _______ tasks can feel _______ for kids.

Many kids ______ _______ well in school.

_______ _______ are fun, but they can also _____ learning.

18 Why Do Prices Change?

음원 듣기

정답: 78쪽

___________ are going up in many places around the world.

Prices change because of ___________ _________ ____________.

If many people ___________ ______________, the price ___________ ______.

For example, ___________ for ice cream ________ _____ in summer.

As a result, ice cream prices ______ _____ by about 25%.

In winter, ice cream ________ _______ because the ___________ is _____.

Businesses _________ prices _____ _________ supply and demand.

That is why prices ________ ______ the same.

E-Scooter Out, Safety In!

정답: 82쪽

_____ _______, over 2,000 e-scooter (electric scooter) accidents happened ____ ________.

In response, Seoul ________ banning e-scooters in some areas _____ ________.

These areas ________ Banpo *hagwon* districts and school zones.

Many students ______ there every day.

The roads are ______ and _____ _______.

But e-scooters can ______ quickly and _______ accidents.

___ people _____ e-scooters in these areas, they _____ ____ __ ____.

This rule helps students walk ______ _______.

정답: 86쪽

20 Need Money to Make Coins!

It's not _________ to make ______ ______ anymore.

Coins _____ _______ ______ different metals, which cost money.

A 10-won coin ______ about 20 won.

That's _______ _______ the coin's value!

___ 2023, _______ prices went up ____ 15%.

So making coins __________ ______ ___________ that year.

Coins are small, but they cost a lot to make.

With costs ________, will we still use coins ___ ______ ________?

MBTI Changes as You Grow!

정답: 90쪽

The MBTI is ___________ with kids these days.

It is ___ ______ that helps them understand _______

______________ .

It also ________ them understand their friends.

However, MBTI types ________ change as they grow.

________________ ____ a study, about 40% of people change

their MBTI type ________ _____ _________ .

MBTI types _____ __________ a lot, especially for

children.

______ _________ is that children change a lot as they

______ .

The MBTI is ______ , but it may not stay _____________ .

UBI: Money Without Work?

정답: 94쪽

Robots and AI are taking __________ _______ today.

So many people ________ ______ their jobs in the future.

Universal basic income, or UBI, is _____________ that may _______.

UBI gives money to all people without them needing to work.

In Finland, _________ __________ got UBI for two years.

They reported that they ______ __________ and tried more new things in their lives.

But some ________ that UBI makes people ______ _______ to work.

UBI can _______ many people, but not everyone _________.

음원 듣기

정답: 98쪽

Korea Needs More Kids!

In 2024, Korea had _____ __________ __________ birth rate.

__________ people are getting _______, and _________ babies are being ______.

Korea is now called ____ _________ _________.

In response, the government is trying _______ to solve this problem.

Some cities help _________ with babies pay rent.

Others give ______ _________ ______ to babies.

Even with this help, the birth rate __________ _____.

_________ __________ are needed to make a real ___________.

The Sharing Economy: Smart or Risky?

More people want to use things __________ buying them.

______ __________ __________ lets people borrow cars, bikes, and homes.

In 2023, over 30% of __________ used sharing services.

Sharing helps people ______ ________ and ________ ________.

But some people ________ about safety and trust.

__________ ________ can feel unsafe to some people.

__________ ______ sometimes get _____ ___ ________ easily.

_____ the sharing economy ______ growing __________.

정답: 106쪽

Words Online Matter, Too!

__________ ______________ ________ are now a big problem.

The Internet helps people ______ _____ _______ ideas easily.

But some words can make others ______ _____ _____ ______.

In 2023, about 15% of __________ felt sad because of ______ ____________.

______________ ________ and _____ ________ can also break _____ _____ in Korea.

Some people _______ _______ to jail for online bullying.

We _______ ____ _________ with our words online.

Words online are ____ ____________ ____ words in real life.

26 Put It in the Bank; Watch It Grow!

정답: 110쪽

Many children today use ______ __________ to save their money.

They ______ ________ in banks to keep it _____ and to help it grow.

Banks give _________, which is __ _______ _______ _________ of money.

In 2024, interest rates in Korea were _________ _____.

Interest helps money grow _______ ____ ______.

Banks also ______ _____ with money plans and saving goals.

That's why _________ ___ __ ______ is the first step for many kids.

It's _______ _________ ______ to learn about ________ ______ __________ money.

Should 16-Year-Olds Vote?

음원 듣기

정답: 114쪽

Today, most countries _____ 18-year-olds _______ in elections.

However, some countries even allow ________________ to vote.

Austria is ______ ____ _______, and it started this rule in 2007.

Some people say ________ ___________ _______ care about the future.

They believe they can _______ smart choices.

Others say ________ ________ ____ need more experience to vote well.

They think the _________ ______ should remain 18.

_______ _________ continues in many countries.

Credit Cards Are Not Free Money

정답: 118쪽

A report says __________ _______ _________ credit cards are used in Korea.

Many people use cards to pay ____________ _______.

Cards make ____________ easy, but they are not _______ _________.

It is ____________ to remember that it is borrowed money.

You __________ _______ ________ the money after using a credit card.

If you pay late, you pay ________ money.

So you __________ _______ _________ not to spend too much.

Cards can be _________, but they must be used _________.

Can Mars Be Our New Earth?

정답: 122쪽

Scientists say the Earth may not last forever.

They say the Earth __________ __________ __________ enough space, food, or water.

That's why Mars explorations __________ __________ __________ __________ these days.

Some people think Mars __________ __________ the next home for __________ .

Elon Musk's company, SpaceX, __________ __________ on this __________ .

It plans to send people to __________ one day.

Others say we __________ __________ the Earth first.

__________ __________ dream about Mars or take care of the Earth __________ ?

Should You Save, Invest, or Both?

정답: 126쪽

Many people want to grow their money for the future.

Some people save money in banks.

Saving ___ ________ but grows money slowly.

Other people ________ their money to grow it ________.

But investing, _____ in stocks or houses, has ______ ____.

For example, in 2023, about 25% of investors _____ ________.

That's why people use ______ ________ _____ __________.

By using both, people _____ ______ their money without too much risk.

MEMO

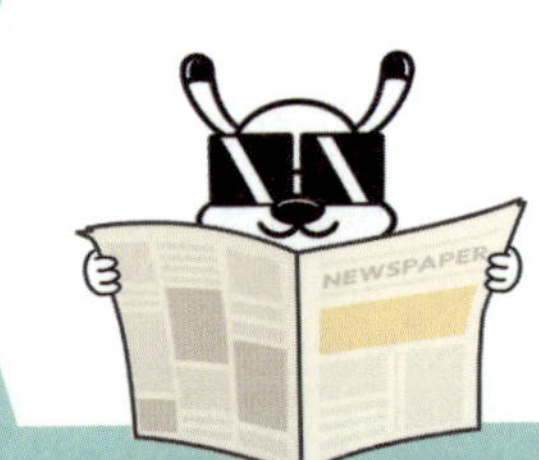

바빠 영어 신문

NEWS TIMES

뉴스 타임스

Answer

① 정답을 확인한 후 틀린 문제는 ★표를 쳐 놓으세요.
② 틀린 문제는 다시 한 번 풀어 보세요.

내가 틀린 문제를 스스로 확인하는 습관을 들이면, 아무리 바쁘더라도 공부 실력을 키울 수 있어요!

01 Social Studies   10쪽

No More Social Media for Kids!

STEP 01

1 ① rule ② strict ③ use

2 ① T ② T

3 law, stop

STEP 03

Main Idea ban

Details ① safe ② harmful ③ strict

Conclusion change

STEP 04

1 No, I don't   **2** Yes, I do

02 Economics   14쪽

Taxes: The Price of a Better Life

STEP 01

1 ① schools ② medicine ③ firefighters

2 ① T ② F

3 Taxes, necessary

STEP 03

Main Idea society

Details ① support ② patients ③ exist

Conclusion better

STEP 04

1 No, I don't   **2** Yes, I do

03 Social Studies   18쪽

AI Is Smart, but People Teach Best

STEP 01

1 ① intelligence ② correctly ③ feelings

2 ① T ② T

3 people, understand

STEP 03

Main Idea replace

Details ① care ② feelings ③ answers

Conclusion useful

STEP 04

1 Yes, I do   **2** No, I don't

04 Economics   22쪽

The Bitcoin Pizza Story

STEP 01

1 ① pizzas ② worth ③ important

2 ① T ② F

3 history, first

STEP 03

Main Idea event

Details ① purchased ② transaction ③ Bitcoin

Conclusion popular

STEP 04

1 No, I don't   **2** Yes, I do

05 Social Studies — 26쪽

Enjoy *Mukbang*, but Stay Healthy!

STEP 01

1 ① popular ② alone ③ mindful

2 ① T ② F

3 careful, habits

STEP 03

Main Idea mindfully

Details ① enjoyable ② much ③ affect

Conclusion watching

STEP 04

1 Yes, I do **2** No, I don't

---

06 Economics — 30쪽

Why Buy New? Shop Smart!

STEP 01

1 ① cheaper ② waste ③ unique

2 ① T ② F

3 secondhand, smart

STEP 03

Main Idea used

Details ① cheaper ② reduces ③ unique

Conclusion smart

STEP 04

1 No, I don't **2** Yes, I do

---

07 Social Studies — 34쪽

No-Kids Zones: Good or Bad?

STEP 01

1 ① quiet ② unfair ③ welcome

2 ① F ② F

3 peaceful, fair

STEP 03

Main Idea different

Details ① adults ② agree ③ take

Conclusion no-kids zones

STEP 04

1 Yes, I do **2** No, I don't

---

08 Economics — 38쪽

Pets Need Insurance, Too

STEP 01

1 ① family ② expensive ③ quickly

2 ① F ② F

3 choosing, smart

STEP 03

Main Idea vet care

Details ① take care of ② medical ③ quickly

Conclusion insurance

STEP 04

1 No, I don't **2** Yes, I do

09 Social Studies · 42쪽

Will Schools Have Fewer Tests?

STEP 01

1 ① tests ② healthy ③ better

2 ① F ② T

3 reduce, exams

STEP 03

Main Idea fewer

Details ① unhealthy ② essays ③ methods

Conclusion replace

STEP 04

1 Yes, I do 2 No, I don't

10 Economics · 46쪽

No Cashier? No Problem?

STEP 01

1 ① Unmanned ② technology ③ convenient

2 ① T ② T

3 stores, cashiers

STEP 03

Main Idea cashiers

Details ① faster ② owners ③ prefer

Conclusion different

STEP 04

1 No, I don't 2 Yes, I do

11 Social Studies · 50쪽

Zoo: Safe Homes or Small Prisons?

STEP 01

1 ① rights ② animals ③ learn

2 ① T ② F

3 attention, care

STEP 03

Main Idea different

Details ① protect ② learn ③ stressed

Conclusion disagree

STEP 04

1 Yes, I do 2 No, I don't

12 Economics · 54쪽

Why Do People Use *Jeonse*?

STEP 01

1 ① unique ② beginning ③ Renters

2 ① F ② F

3 *jeonse*, homeowners

STEP 03

Main Idea renters

Details ① monthly ② rent ③ investments

Conclusion *jeonse*

STEP 04

1 No, I don't 2 Yes, I do

13   Social Studies   58쪽

Do You Want to Be a YouTuber?

STEP 01

1 ① YouTubers   ② hobbies   ③ videos

2 ① F   ② T

3 Being, before

STEP 03

Main Idea easy

Details ① videos   ② stressed   ③ bully

Conclusion carefully

STEP 04

1 Yes, I do   2 No, I don't

14   Economics   62쪽

Brands: More Than Just a Name

STEP 01

1 ① buy   ② who   ③ advertising

2 ① F   ② T

3 important, affect

STEP 03

Main Idea what

Details ① choose   ② images   ③ money

Conclusion Brand

STEP 04

1 No, I don't   2 Yes, I do

15   Social Studies   66쪽

Why Do We Have to Go to School?

STEP 01

1 ① School   ② skills   ③ work

2 ① T   ② F

3 teamwork, communication skill

STEP 03

Main Idea well

Details ① practice   ② responsibility   ③ jobs

Conclusion important

STEP 04

1 Yes, I do   2 No, I don't

16   Economics   70쪽

Game Money Is for Games Only!

STEP 01

1 ① money   ② In-game   ③ real

2 ① F   ② T

3 own, game

STEP 03

Main Idea inside

Details ① popular   ② games   ③ outside

Conclusion same

STEP 04

1 No, I don't   2 Yes, I do

17　Social Studies　74쪽

Short Videos, Short Focus

STEP 01

1 ① survey　② minute　③ learn
2 ① F　② F
3 short, attention

STEP 03

Main Idea Watching
Details ① shorten　② harder　③ focus
Conclusion careful

STEP 04

1 No, I don't　2 Yes, I do

18　Economics　78쪽

Why Do Prices Change?

STEP 01

1 ① price　② up　③ Businesses
2 ① F　② T
3 Prices, supply

STEP 03

Main Idea demand
Details ① more　② expensive　③ cheaper
Conclusion control

STEP 04

1 No, I don't　2 Yes, I do

19　Social Studies　82쪽

E-Scooter Out, Safety In!

STEP 01

1 ① accidents　② areas　③ fine
2 ① T　② T
3 rule, students

STEP 03

Main Idea banning
Details ① Many　② accidents　③ use
Conclusion safely

STEP 04

1 Yes, I do　2 No, I don't

20　Economics　86쪽

Need Money to Make Coins!

STEP 01

1 ① costs　② cheap　③ metals
2 ① F　② F
3 coins, more

STEP 03

Main Idea coins
Details ① metals　② costs　③ cheap
Conclusion expensive

STEP 04

1 No, I don't　2 Yes, I do

21 · Social Studies — 90쪽

MBTI Changes as You Grow!

STEP 01

1 ① test ② change ③ understand

2 ① T ② F

3 Children, older

STEP 03

Main Idea same

Details ① personality ② time ③ change

Conclusion fixed

STEP 04

1 Yes, I do   2 No, I don't

22 · Economics — 94쪽

UBI: Money Without Work?

STEP 01

1 ① jobs ② happier ③ lazy

2 ① T ② F

3 everyone, work

STEP 03

Main Idea UBI

Details ① technologies ② money ③ working

Conclusion disagree

STEP 04

1 Yes, I do   2 No, I don't

23 · Social Studies — 98쪽

Korea Needs More Kids!

STEP 01

1 ① babies ② aging society ③ health care

2 ① F ② F

3 birth rate, changes

STEP 03

Main Idea lowest

Details ① children ② older ③ solve

Conclusion raise

STEP 04

1 Yes, I do   2 No, I don't

24 · Economics — 102쪽

The Sharing Economy: Smart or Risky?

STEP 01

1 ① sharing ② money ③ safety

2 ① F ② T

3 borrow, save

STEP 03

Main Idea economy

Details ① buying ② waste ③ worry

Conclusion useful

STEP 04

1 No, I don't   2 Yes, I do

29 Social Studies 122쪽

Can Mars Be Our New Earth?

STEP 01

1 ① Earth ② Mars ③ explorations

2 ① F ② F

3 living, protect

STEP 03

Main Idea home

Details ① last ② answer ③ save

Conclusion agrees

STEP 04

1 No, I don't **2** Yes, I do

30 Economics 126쪽

Should You Save, Invest, or Both?

STEP 01

1 ① save ② invest ③ safer

2 ① F ② T

3 saving, investing (순서 상관없음)

STEP 03

Main Idea grow

Details ① slowly ② risk ③ investing

Conclusion both

STEP 04

1 Yes, I do **2** No, I don't

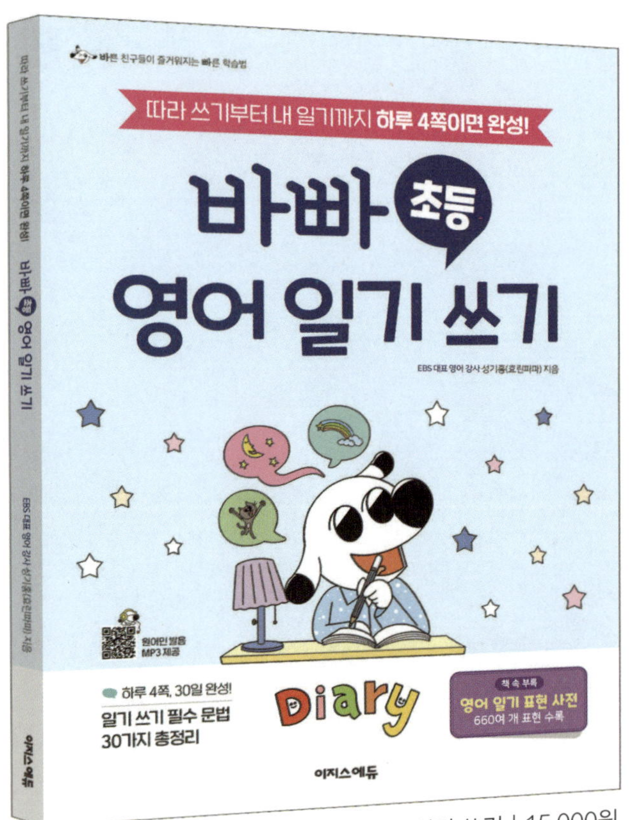

바빠 초등 영어 일기 쓰기 | 15,000원

매일 4쪽씩, 30일 완성!
초등 영어
일기 쓰기

EBS 대표 영어 강사
효린파파 집필!

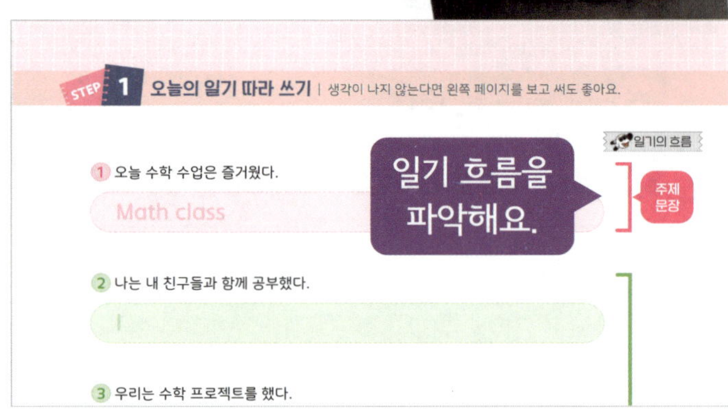

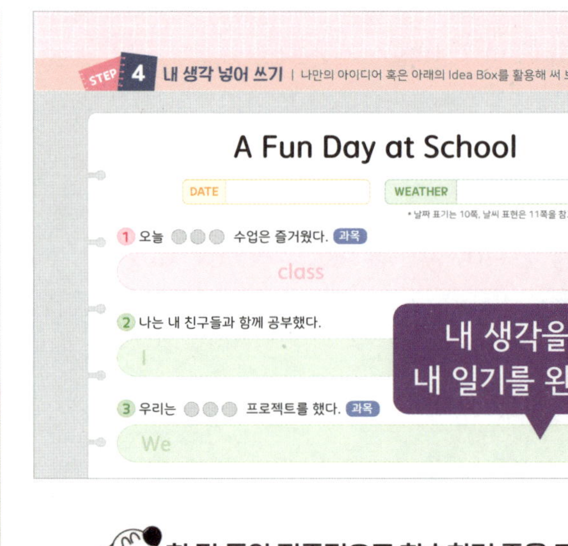
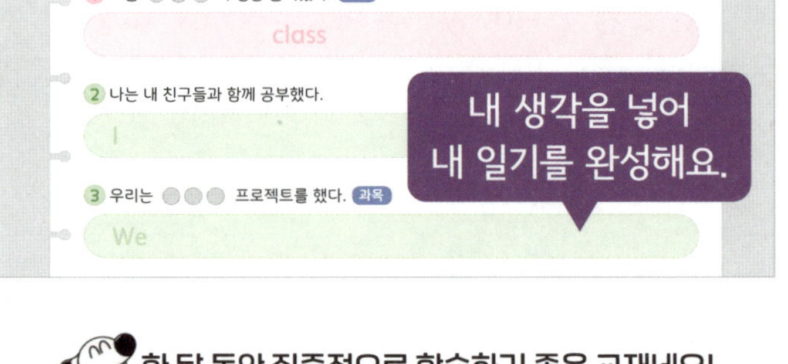

한 달 동안 집중적으로 학습하기 좋은 교재네요!